Shaping the European Mind

Intellectual Trends in Modern Europe ...From the Renaissance to the 20th Century

Paul Dykes & John C. Powell

NEW FORUMS PRESS INC.
Stillwater, Okla., U.S.A.

Copyright © 2003 by Paul Dykes and John C. Powell

All rights reserved. No part of this publication may be reproduced or transmitted in any form or by any means, electronic or mechanical, including photocopy, or any information storage or retrieval system, without permission in writing from the publisher.

This book may be ordered in bulk quantities at discount from New Forums Press, Inc., P.O. Box 876, Stillwater, OK 74076 [Federal I.D. No. 73 1123239]. Printed in the United States of America.

International Standard Book Number: 1-58107-081-0

TABLE OF CONTENTS

Introduction ix

PART ONE 1
  MACHIAVELLI 3
    The Prince (1532 5
    I—Of Princedoms Won by Merit 5
    II—Of Princedoms Won Otherwise than by Merit 6
    III—Of Maintaining A Princedom 8
    IV—Of Artifices 10
  ERASMUS 12
    Praise of Folly (1511) 14
  LUTHER 16
    Martin Luther Discovers Justification by Faith 18
    Luther Calls on the German Nobility to Reform The Church .. 20
    German Peasants Protest Rising Feudal Exactions 21
  CALVIN 23
    Calvin's Institutes of the Christian Religion 25
  HENRY VIII 27
    The Act of Supremacy (1534) 29
    The King's Grace to be Authorized Supreme Head ... 29
  SIR THOMAS MORE 30
    Sir Thomas More's Utopia (1516) 32
    —Of the Island of Utopia and the Customs of its People . 32
    —Of the Wars and the Religion of the Utopians 34
  ZWINGLI 37
    Zwingli Criticizes the Catholic Church 38
  LOYOLA 40
    Loyola's Rules for the Jesuits 41
  HENRY IV 43
    The Edict of Nantes 45

PART TWO 47

- Mercantilism 49
- JAMES I 50
  - James I on the Divine Right of Kings 51
- CHARLES I 52
  - The Parliament Petitions Charles I 54
- CROMWELL 55
  - Description of Oliver Cromwell by the Earl of Clarendon 57
  - The Execution of Charles I, (1649) 59
- HOBBES 61
  - Thomas Hobbes' Leviathan 63
    - I-Of Man 63
    - II-Of Contract and Sovereignty 65
    - III-The Natural Commonwealth 67
    - IV-Of A Christian Commonwealth 70
- WILLIAM AND MARY 72
  - The English Bill of Rights 74
- LOCKE 76
  - An Essay Concerning Human Understanding 77
    - I-The Nature of Simple Ideas 77
    - II-Of Idea-Producing Qualities 79
    - III-Various Faculties of the Mind 80
    - IX-Our Knowledge of the Existence of Other Things 82
- RICHELIEU 85
  - Richelieu's Political Will and Testament 86
- BOSSUET 88
  - Bossuet on the Divine Right of Kings 89
  - Saint Simon on Louis XIV 90
- LOUIS XIV 91
  - Louis XIV on His Role as King 92

PART THREE	**93**
COPERNICUS	95
Copernicus on the Movement of the Earth	96
GALILEO	98
Galileo on Science and the Bible (1615)	99
BACON	101
Novum Organum	102
NEWTON	105
Newton's Rules of Reasoning (1687	107
PASCAL	109
Pascal on Thinking Creatures	110
DESCARTES	111
Descartes' Discourse on Methods	112
I—The Aim of the Discourse	112
II—The Intellectual Crises	113
III—A Rule of Life	115
IV—'I Think, Therefore I Am'	116
V-Why I do not Publish 'The World'	119
SPINOZA	122
Spinoza's On the Improvement of the Understanding	123
KANT	128
Kant's Fundamental Principles of the Metaphysic of Morals	129
MONTESQUIEU	136
Montesquieu's Spirit of the Laws	138
VOLTAIRE	140
Voltaire on Religion	142
Voltaire's Support of Enlightened Despotism	144
ROUSSEAU	146
Rousseau's The Social Contract (1726	148
I—The Terms of the Compact	148
II—The Sovereign and the Laws	150
III—The Government	151
SMITH	155
Wealth of Nations	157

PART FOUR 159
   Demands of the Third Estate 161
   The Declaration of the Rights of Man and Citizen (1789 163
   BURKE 166
   Burke's Reflections on the French Revolution (1790) 167
   PAINE 168
   Paine's The Rights of Man (1790 and 1792) 169
      I—Natural and Civil Rights 169
      II—France and England Compared 171
      III—The Old and New Systems 173
      IV—The Reform of England 175
   WOLLSTONECRAFT 178
   Wollstonecraft's A Vindication of the
      Rights of Women (1792) 179
   The Consuls Declare the Revolution Over 181

PART FIVE 183
   MALTHUS 185
   On the Principle of Population 185
      I-General Survey of the Checks to Population ....
      II-Population and the Subsistence Level ....
      III-Remedies Other Than Moral for Over-Population ....
      IV-Moral Restraint and Discriminate Charity ....
   MARX 196
   The Communist Manifesto (1848 197
   ENGELS 201
   Engel's On the Plight of the Worker 202
   DE TOCQUEVILLE 203
   De Tocqueville on the June Revolution 204
   DARWIN 205
   Darwin's View of Nature 207
   BISMARCK 209
   The Ems Dispatch (1870) 211

MAZZINI 213
    Mazzini Pleads for Italian Unity 214
    The Role of Race, by H.S. Chamberlain 215
KIPLING 216
    Kipling Advises the Americans 217
ZOLA 219
    "I Accuse" 220
MILL 224
    Utilitarianism 225
NIETZSCHE 234
    Beyond Good and Evil 235

PART SIX **241**
LENIN 243
    The Fourteen Points 244
    Lenin's April Thesis 248
    Lenin as Dictator 250
MUSSOLINI 251
    Mussolini on Fascism 253
CHURCHILL 256
    Churchill on the Munich Agreement 258
    Churchill's Iron Curtain Speech (1946) 259
HITLER 261
    Nazi Racial Policy 262
    A Description of the Holocaust 264
TRUMAN 266
    The Truman Doctrine (1947) 267
KRUSCHEV 269
    Kruschev Denounces Stalin 271
50 Great Paintings 273
10 Great Composers 275
75 Words to Study History with 276

Introduction

This text is designed to introduce readers to some of the main currents of European thought from the Renaissance to the modern era. While not comprehensive, it includes some of the most influential thinkers of the modern era. It is the opinion of the editors that exposure to these primary sources will enhance one's study of European history. The editors take full responsibility for any omissions that have occurred or for any errors that have taken place in the editing process.

The biographical sketches that accompany these documents are designed to help students place each source in its proper context. Readers are urged to contemplate why, when, where, and how these words were first delivered. In some cases students may discern that the cares and concerns of those who have gone before us are not substantially different from our own concerns. It is the aim of the text for readers to see how these words have influenced the modern world.

We thank Heritage Hall of Oklahoma City for providing the support that made this publication possible. The readings reflect the convictions of those who wrote them. We encourage attention to the selections; agreement or disagreement is the option of the reader.

Dr. John C. Powell
Chair Social Studies Dept.
Heritage Hall
Oklahoma City, Oklahoma

Paul Dykes
English Faculty
Booker T. Washington H.S.
Tulsa, Oklahoma

Shaping the European Mind

PART ONE

NICCOLO MACHIAVELLI

(1469-1527)

"A Prince must avoid being despised as well as being hated; therefore courage, wisdom and strength must be apparent in all his actions."

Machiavelli was born in Florence, Italy, in 1469. At the time Italy did not exist as a nation; rather, the Italian peninsula was organized politically by a series of city states. Rivalries among the city states and outside forces were substantial. Machiavelli was employed by the Florentine Republic to handle diplomatic negotiations and to supervise certain military operations of the state. This role in Florentine politics gave Machiavelli the opportunity to work closely with heads of states and to observe their tactics and behaviors. When the Medici regained power in Florence in 1512, Machiavelli found himself out of a job and in prison on charges of disloyalty. Although he never returned to prominence in Florence, during his political exile Machiavelli conceived his great work, *The Prince*.

Machiavelli has often been called the first political scientist. His political theory is based on the cutthroat politics of Renaissance Italy and comprises an entirely secular approach to government. Machiavelli states that a prince is not bound by ethical (moral) traditions and should create policy based on one central criterion: *the good of the state*. Machiavelli sees the state and the prince as one. Since their interests are inextricably bound, Machiavelli assumes all decisions made by the prince advance the good of the state.

Machiavellian politics has become synonymous with modern political theory. While *The Prince* was not published during Machiavelli's lifetime, its influence has been substantial. His advice has inspired political leaders from virtually every era since the publication of *The Prince* in 1532. It seems his work has become standard reading for those who aspire to power.

(The Italian Renaissance contributed to a more secular view of the world. Governments began to adopt this secular view. Niccolo Machiavelli, in The Prince, *published in 1532, rationalized that moral principles must give way to expediency. It is the Prince that must make these decisions. Machiavelli's rationale greatly influenced the governments of Europe.)*

THE PRINCE (1532)
NICCOLO MACHIAVELLI

I-Of Princedoms Won by Merit

All states and governments are either republics or princedoms. Princedoms are either hereditary or new. Hereditary states are maintained with far less difficulty than new states, but in new princedoms difficulties abound.

And first if the princedom be joined on to ancient dominions of the prince, so as to form a mixed princedom, rebellion is a danger, for men are always ready to change masters. When a state rebels and is again got under, it will not afterwards be lost so easily; for the prince will use the rebellion as a pretext to make himself more secure.

In such provinces, moreover, the prince should always make himself the protector of his weaker neighbors, without adding to their strength; but should humble the great, and never suffer a formidable stranger to acquire influence, as was the rule with the Romans. Whereas King Louis of France has in Italy done the direct opposite in every single respect. In especial we may draw from the French king's actions the general axiom, which never or rarely errs, that "he who is the cause of another's greatness is himself undone".

Now, all princedoms are governed in one of two ways: either by a sole prince served by ministers, or by a prince with barons who hold their rank not by favor but by right of descent. The Turk is an example of the first, the French king of the second. A state of the first kind is difficult to win, but when won is easily held, since the prince's family may be easily rooted out; but in such a state as France you may gain an entry, but to hold your ground afterwards is difficult, since you cannot root out the barons.

Hence we need not wonder at the ease wherewith Alexander was able to lay a firm hold on Asia; albeit he died before he had well entered on possession; since the dominion of Darius was of the same character as that of the Turk.

When the newly acquired state has hitherto lived under its own laws and in freedom there are three ways of holding it. The first is to destroy it; the second to reside in it; the third to leave it under its own laws, choosing for its governors from the inhabitants such as will be friendly to you. But the safest course is either to destroy it or to go and live in it.

Where the prince himself is new, either merit or good fortune is implied, and if we consider the most excellent examples, such as Moses, Cyrus, Romulus and the like, we shall see that they owed to fortune nothing beyond the opportunity which they seized. Those who, like these, come to the princedom by virtuous paths acquire with difficulty, but keep with ease. Their difficulties arise because they are of necessity innovators. If, then, they have force of their own to employ, they seldom fail. Hence it comes that all armed prophets have been victorious and all unarmed prophets have been destroyed; as was the case with Savonarola.

II-Of Princedoms Won Otherwise than by Merit

Those who rise to princedom by mere good fortune have much trouble to maintain themselves; some lack both knowledge and the power to do. Yet even if such a one be of great parts, he may lose what he has won, like Cesare Borgia.

It was impossible for the duke to aggrandise himself unless the states of Italy were thrown into confusion so that he might safely make himself master of some part of them. This was made easy for him as concerned Romagna by the conduct of the French and Venetians. The next step was to weaken the factions of the Orsini and the Colonnesi. Having scattered the Colonnesi, the Orsini were so won over as to be drawn in their simplicity into his hands at Sinigaglia. Having thus disposed of the leaders, he set about ingratiating himself with the population of Romagna and Urbino. He first set over the country a stern ruler to restore order. This end being accomplished, that stern but unpopular ruler was beheaded. Next, as a new pope might be dangerous, he set himself to exterminate the kindred of those lords whom he had despoiled of their possessions, to win over the Roman nobility, and to secure a majority among the cardinals. But before the duke had completely consolidated his power his father, Pope Alexander VI, died. Even so, the skills with which he had laid the foundations of his power must have resulted in success had he not himself been almost at death's door at that critical moment. The one mistake he made was in the choice of the new pope, Julius II, and this error was the cause of his ultimate downfall.

A man may rise, however, to a princedom by paths of wickedness and crime; that is, not precisely by either merit or fortune. We may take as example first Agathocles the Sicilian. To slaughter fellow citizens, to betray friends, to be devoid of honour, pity and religion cannot be counted as merit. But the achievements of Agathocles can certainly not be ascribed to fortune. We cannot, therefore, attribute either to fortune or to merit what he accomplished without either.

For a modern instance we may consider Oliverotto of Fermo, who seized upon that town by a piece of monstrous treachery and merciless butchery; yet he established himself so firmly that he could not have been unseated had he not let himself be over-reached by Cesare Borgia.

Our lesson from these examples is that on seizing a state the usurper should make haste to inflict what injuries he must at one stroke, and afterwards win men over by benefits.

Next is the case of those who are made princes by the favor of their countrymen, which they owe to what may be termed a fortunate astuteness. If he be established by the favor of the people, to secure them against the oppression of the nobles, his position is stronger than if he owe it to the nobles; but in either case it is the people whom he must conciliate, and this I affirm in spite of the old saw, "He who builds on the people builds on mire".

Merit, or good fortune, is needed to acquire ecclesiastical princedoms, but not to maintain them, for they are upheld by the authority of religion. It is due to the policy of the Popes Alexander VI and Julius II that the temporal power of the pope has become so great; and from his holiness Pope Leo we may hope that as his predecessors made the papacy great with arms he will render it still greater and more venerable by his benignity and other countless virtues.

III-Of Maintaining a Princedom

A prince must defend his state with either his own subjects or mercenaries, or auxiliaries. Mercenaries are utterly untrustworthy; if their captain be not an able man the prince will probably be ruined, whereas if he be an able man he will be seeking a goal of his own. This has been perpetually exemplified among the cities and states of Italy which have sought to maintain themselves by taking foreigners into their pay.

But he who would deprive himself of every chance of success should have recourse to auxiliaries; that is, to the troops of a foreign potentate. For these are far more dangerous than mercenary arms, bringing ruin with them ready made. The better such troops are the more dangerous they are. From Hiero of Syracuse to Cesare Borgia, princes have become powerful in proportion as they could dispense with such aid and place their dependence upon national troops.

A prince, then, who would be powerful should have no care or thought but for war, lest he lose his dominions. If he be ignorant of military affairs he can neither be respected by the soldiers nor trust them. Therefore, he must both practise and study this art. For the practise, the chase in many respects provides an excellent training both in knowledge of the country and in vigor of the body. As to study, a prince should read histories, note the actions of great men and examine the causes of their victories and defeats, imitating those who have been renowned.

Anyone who would act up to a perfect standard of goodness in everything must be ruined among so many who are not good. It is essential, therefore, for a prince to have learnt how to be other than good and to use, or not to use, his goodness as necessity requires.

It may be a good thing to be reputed liberal, but liberality without the reputation of it is hurtful. Display necessitates the imposition of taxes, whereby the prince becomes hateful; whereas through parsimony his revenue will be sufficient. Hence we have seen no princes accomplish great results save those who have been accounted miserly by the world.

Every prince should desire to be accounted merciful, not cruel; but a new prince cannot escape a name for cruelty, for he who quells disorder by a few signal examples will, in the end, be the more merciful.

Men are less careful how they offend him who makes himself loved than him who makes himself feared; yet should a prince inspire fear in such a fashion that, if he do not win love, he may escape hate; remember that men will sooner forget the slaying of their father than the loss of their patrimony.

Princes who set little store by their word but have known how to overreach men by their cunning have accomplished great things, and in the end got the better of those who trusted to honest dealing. The prince must be a lion, but he must also know how to play the fox. He who wishes to deceive will never fail to find willing dupes. The prince, in short, ought not to quit good courses if he can help it, but should know how to follow evil courses if he must.

A prince must avoid being despised as well as being hated; therefore courage, wisdom and strength must be apparent in all his actions. Against such a one conspiracy is difficult. That prince is wise who devolves on others those matters that entail responsibility, and may therefore make him odious either to the nobles or to the commons, but reserves to himself the matters that relate to grace and favour.

What I have said is not contradicted by the history of the Roman emperors; for they had to choose between satisfying the soldiers and satisfying the people. It was imperative that at any cost they should maintain control of the soldiery, which scarce any of them could do without injustice to the people. If we examine their histories we shall find that they fully bear out the principles I have laid down.

But in our time the standing armies of princes have not the same power as the armies of the Roman Empire, and except under the Turk and the Soldan it is more needful to satisfy the people than to satisfy the soldiery.

IV-Of Artifices

A new prince will never disarm his subjects, but will rather arm them, at least in part. For thus they become his partisans, whereas without them he must depend on mercenaries.

But a prince who adds a new state to his old possessions should disarm its inhabitants, relying on the soldiers of his own ancient dominions. Some have fostered feuds among their new subjects in order to keep them weak, but such a policy rarely proves useful in the end. The prince who acquires a new state will gain more strength by winning over and trusting those who were at first opposed to him than by relying on those who were at first his friends.

The prince who is more afraid of his subjects than of strangers ought to build fortresses, while he who is more afraid of strangers than of his subjects should leave them alone. The best fortress you can have is in not being hated by your subjects.

Nothing makes a prince so well thought of as to undertake great enterprises and give striking proofs of his capacity. Ferdinand of Aragon, in our own time, has become the foremost king in Christendom. If you consider his achievements, you will find them all great and some extraordinary. First he made war on Granada, and this was the foundation of his power. Under the cloak of religion, with what may be called pious cruelty, he cleared his kingdom of the Moors, made war on Africa, invaded Italy and finally attacked France; while his subjects, occupied with these great actions, had neither time nor opportunity to oppose them.

To retain a good minister the prince will bind him to himself by benefits. Above all, he will avoid being deceived by flatterers, and while he consults his counsellors should reflect and judge for himself. A prince who is not wise himself cannot be well advised by others.

The Italian princes who in our own times have lost their dominions have either been deficient in respect of arms, or have had the people against them, or have not known how to secure themselves against the nobles. As to the influence of fortune it may be the case that she is the mistress of one half of our actions, but leaves the control of the other half to ourselves. That prince will prosper most whose mode of acting best adapts itself to the character of the times; so that at one time a cautious temperament, and at another an impetuous temperament, will be the more successful.

Now, at this time the whole land of Italy is without a head, without order, beaten, spoiled, torn in pieces, overrun, and abandoned to destruction in every shape. She prays God to send someone to rescue her from these barbarous cruelties; she is eager to follow anyone who could undertake the part of a deliverer: nor does this seem too hard a task for you, the Magnificent Lorenzo of the illustrious house of Medici. The cause is just; we have before us unexampled proofs of Divine favour. Everything has concurred to promote your greatness. What remains to be done must be done by you, for God will not do everything Himself.

(From an 18th century translation of *The Prince*)

DESIDERUS ERASMUS

(1466-1536)

"Almost all Christians are wretchedly enslaved to blindness and ignorance, which the priests are so far from preventing or removing that they blacken the darkness and promote the delusion....."

Ersasmus was born in Rotterdam (Netherlands) in 1466. The illegitimate son of a priest, Erasmus was educated in the strict scholastic tradition. Although trained as an Augustinian scholar, Erasmus is best known as a teacher and writer. Around 1499 Erasmus took up the life of a traveling scholar and visited many of the great cities of Europe. One of his most productive periods was in England where he met and worked with the English scholar Thomas More. Erasmus was a master of the classical texts and through them developed a strong humanist philosophy based upon naturalism, tolerance, and the call for a more humane treatment of mankind. Erasmus was convinced of the inherent goodness of man and began to question the dogmatism of the church.

Erasmus's most important work was his satire *The Praise of Folly*. His goal was to expose the corruption and inconsistency of the Catholic Church by using humor and irony. Because he employed a more indirect attack on the abuses of the church, he was tolerated and even lauded as a man of integrity by church officials. His main message focused on the return to the simple teachings of Christ. After 1517, things began to change for Erasmus. Martin Luther's direct attacks on the Catholic hierarchy created a backlash against those who would criticize church authorities. Erasmus's last days were spent in virtual exile within Catholic Europe, as his style was branded as dangerous and even heretical.

Erasmus's influence on Luther was considerable. He opened the door for criticism of the Catholic Church and found the door impossible to close. In sum, however, he should be remembered as one of the foremost advocates of humanist philosophy in the sixteenth century.

(The Renaissance placed great importance on the development of man and his own power and virtue. Humanism stressed human activity, and the need for man to improve himself. Christian Humanists, such as Desiderius Erasmus, attacked the church for its narrow vision and ignorance. Because he used satire and humor, Erasmus was never condemned by the church. Furthermore, he sought a Catholic Reformation, and not a total break with the church.)

PRAISE OF FOLLY (1511)
DESIDERIUS ERASMUS

Almost all Christians are wretchedly enslaved to blindness and ignorance, which the priests are so far from preventing or removing that they blacken the darkness and promote the delusion; wisely foreseeing that the people (like cows, which never give down their milk so well as when they are gently stroked) would part with less if they knew more, their bounty proceeding only from a mistake of charity. Now if any grave, wise man should stand up and unseasonably speak the truth, telling everyone that a pious life is the only way of securing a happy death; that the best title to a pardon of our sins is purchased by a hearty abhorrence of our guilt, and sincere resolutions of amendment; that the best devotion which can be paid to any saints is to imitate them in their exemplary life; if he should proceed thus to inform them of their several mistakes, there would be quite another estimate put upon tears, watchings, masses, fastings, and other severities, which before were so much prized, as persons will now be vexed to lose that satisfaction they formerly found in them....

Next come the philosophers, with their long beards and short cloaks, who esteem themselves as the only favorites of wisdom, and look upon the rest of mankind as the dirt and rubbish of the creation; yet these men's happiness is only a frantic craziness of brain. They build castles in the air, and infinite worlds in a vacuum. They will give you to a hair's breadth the dimensions of the sun, moon, and stars, as easily as they would that of a flagon or pipkin; they will give an elaborate account of the cause of thunder, of the origin of the winds, of the nature of eclipses, and of the most abstruse difficulties in physics, without the least demur or hesitation, as if they had been admitted into the cabinet council of nature, or had been eye-witnesses to all the methods of creation; though in fact nature does but laugh at all their puny conjectures; for they never yet made one considerable discovery, as appears from the fact that on no single point of the smallest moment have they unanimously agreed; nothing being so plain or evident but that by someone it is opposed and contradicted....

The divines present themselves next; but it may perhaps be most safe to pass them by, and not to touch upon so harsh a string as this subject would afford. Besides, the undertaking may be very hazardous, for they are a sort of men generally very hot and passionate; and should I provoke them, they would no doubt set upon me with a cry and force me with shame to recant. If I stubbornly refused to do this, they would presently brand me for a heretic, and thunder out an excommunication, which is their spiritual weapon to wound such as lift up a hand against them.

Now as to the popes of Rome who pretend to be Christ's vicars: If they would but imitate his exemplary life in being employed in an unintermitting course of preaching; in being attended with poverty, nakedness, hunger, and a contempt of this world; if they did but consider the import of the word Pope, which signifies a father; or if they did but practice their surname of most holy, what order or degrees of men would be in a worse condition?

All their riches, all their honors, their jurisdictions, their Peter's patrimony, their offices, their dispensations, their licenses, their indulgences, their long train of attendants (see in how short a compass I have abbreviated all their marketing of religion); in a word, all their perquisites would be forfeited and lost; and in their room would succeed watchings, fasting, tears, prayers, sermons, hard studies, repenting sighs, and a thousand such like severe penalties: nay, what is still more deplorable, it would then follow that all their clerks, amanuenses, notaries, advocates, proctors, secretaries, the offices of grooms, hostlers, serving men (and something else, which for modesty's sake I shall not mention); in short, all these troops of attendants which depend on his holiness would all lose their respective employments.

MARTIN LUTHER

(1483-1546)

"For the word of God cannot be received and honored by any works, but by faith alone."

Martin Luther was born in 1483 in the German state of Saxony, one of several hundred such German principalities which existed in the fifteenth century. The son of a miner, Luther attended the University of Wittenberg and received a doctorate in theology. In 1505 Luther underwent a religious conversion significant enough for him to begin questioning some of the basic tenets of Catholic theology. The exact nature of this experience is not clear to us; Luther described his experience as a flash or bolt of lightning. Lutheran tradition has it that Luther was struck dumb during a fierce thunderstorm while on the road. Luther tells us a somewhat different story, in that he tells us his insight came while sitting on the privy. The version of the story is less important than the result. Luther's questioning eventually led to an outright break with the Catholic Church.

The immediate event that led Luther to his radical position was the selling of indulgences by a Catholic priest by the name of Tetzel. Luther adopted the position that salvation was not something that could be dispensed by the church, but was, rather, a result of individual faith. His heavy emphasis on personal interpretation of the scriptures led him to challenge Tetzel and the church on the indulgence issue. In 1517, Luther posted his *Ninety-Five Theses* on a church door in Wittenberg. Initially these "protests" were intended as a call for reform. In time the *Ninety-Five Theses* would form the basis for a complete break with the Catholic Church. Protected by certain German princes, most notably the Duke of Saxony, Luther's heretical views spread through much of Northern Europe.

Luther stands as the foremost catalyst of the Protestant movement. 1517 marks the point at which Catholic Europe would see the end of the universal church in Western Europe. Many peasants interpreted Luther's message of salvation by faith alone as a call for political (secular) freedom. Luther makes clear in his *Address to the German Nobility* that he did not speak to secular authority, and subsequently called for violent oppression of the peasant revolts of the 1520's in Northern Europe.

(Martin Luther must be considered the central figure in the Reformation era. His religious conviction was based upon the concept of justification through faith.)

Martin Luther Discovers Justification by Faith

Though I lived as a monk without reproach, I felt that I was a sinner before God with an extremely disturbed conscience. I could not believe that he was placated by my satisfaction. I did not love, yes, I hated the righteous God who punishes sinners, and secretly, if not blasphemously, certainly murmuring greatly, I was angry with God, and said, "As if, indeed, it is not enough, that miserable sinners, eternally lost through original sin, are crushed by every kind of calamity by the law of the decalogue, without having God add pain to pain by the gospel and also by the gospel threatening us with his righteousness and wrath!" Thus I raged with a fierce and troubled conscience. Nevertheless, I beat importunately upon Paul at that place, most ardently desiring to know what St. Paul wanted.

At last, by the mercy of God, meditating day and night, I gave heed to the context of the words, namely, "In it the righteousness of God is revealed, as it is written, 'He who through faith is righteous shall live'" [Romans 1:17]. There I began to understand that the righteousness of God is that by which the righteous lives by a gift of God, namely by faith. And this is the meaning: the righteousness of God is revealed by the gospel, namely, the passive righteousness with which merciful God justifies us by faith, as it is written; here I felt that I was altogether born again and had entered paradise itself through open gates. There a totally other face of the entire Scripture showed itself to me. Thereupon I ran through the Scriptures from memory. I also found in other terms an analogy, as, the work of God, that is, what God does in us, the power of God, with which he makes us strong, the wisdom of God, with which he makes us wise, the strength of God, the salvation of God, the glory of God.

And I extolled my sweetest word with a love as great as the hatred with which I had before hated the word "righteousness of God." Thus that place in Paul was for me truly the gate to paradise. (From Luther's writings-1545)

(By calling upon the nobility to reform the Church, Luther helped create the religious conflict which troubled Europe throughout the sixteenth century.)

Luther Calls on the German Nobility to Reform The Church

In his *Address to the Christian Nobility of the German Nation* (1520), Luther protested against the three "walls" of Rome that had prevented reform in the church by making the pope immune to corrective action on the basis of secular, biblical, and conciliar authority. In the following, Luther urges the nobility to tear down these walls.

The Romanists have with great dexterity built around themselves three walls, which hitherto have protected themselves [from] reform; and thereby is Christianity fearfully fallen.

In the first place, when the temporal power has pressed them hard [to reform], they have... maintained that the temporal power has no jurisdiction over them, that, on the contrary, the spiritual [power] is above the temporal.

Secondly, when it was proposed to admonish them from the Holy Scriptures they said, "It befits no one but the pope to interpret the Scriptures."

And, thirdly, when they were threatened with a council, they invented the idea that no one but the pope can call a council.

Thus have they secretly stolen our three rods so that they may go unpunished, and entrenched themselves safely behind these three walls in order to carry on all the knavery and wickedness that we now see....

Now may God help us, and give us one of those trumpets that overthrew the walls of Jericho, so that we may also blow down these walls of straw and paper and...regain possession of our Christian rods for the chastisement of sin and expose the craft and deceit of the Devil.

(James Harvey Robinson (Ed.), *Readings in European History*, Vol. 2 Boston: Ginn and Co., 1906)

(The German peasants in the late fifteenth and early sixteenth centuries demanded greater personal freedom from the nobility. The following grievances are representative of the peasants' viewpoints.)

German Peasants Protest Rising Feudal Exactions

1. It is our humble petition and desire...that in the future...each community should choose and appoint a pastor, and that we should have the right to depose him should he conduct himself improperly....
2. We are ready and willing to pay the fair tithe of grain.... The small tithes [of cattle], whether [to] ecclesiastical or lay lords, we will not pay at all, for the Lord God created cattle for the free use of man....
3. We...take it for granted that you will release us from serfdom as true Christians, unless it should be shown us from the Gospel that we are serfs.
4. It has been the custom heretofore that no poor man should be allowed to catch venison or wildfowl or fish in flowing water, which seems to us quite unseemly and unbrotherly as well as selfish and not agreeable to the Word of God....
5. We are aggrieved in the matter of woodcutting, for the noblemen have appropriated all the woods to themselves....
6. In regard to the excessive services demanded of us which are increased from day to day, we ask that this matter be properly looked into so that we shall not continue to be oppressed in this way....
7. We will not hereafter allow ourselves to be further oppressed by our lords, but will let them demand only what is just and proper according to the word of the agreement between the lord and the peasant. The lord should no longer try to force more services or other dues from the peasant without payment....
8. We are greatly burdened because our holdings cannot support the rent extracted from them.... We ask that the lords may appoint persons of honor to inspect these holdings and fix a rent in accordance with justice....

9. We are burdened with a great evil in the constant making of new laws.... In our opinion we should be judged according to the old written law....
10. We are aggrieved by the appropriation...of meadows and fields which at one time belonged to a community as a whole. These we will take again into our own hands....
11. We will entirely abolish the due called Todfall [that is, heriot or death tax, by which the lord received the best horse, cow, or garment of a family upon the death of a serf] and will no longer endure it, nor allow widows and orphans to be thus shamefully robbed against God's will, and in violation of justice and right.
12. It is our conclusion and final resolution, that if any one or more of the articles here set forth should not be in agreement with the Word of God, as we think they are, such article we will willingly retract.

(Translations and Reprints from the Original Sources of European History, Vol. 2, Philadelphia: Department of History, University of Pennsylvania, 1897)

JOHN CALVIN

(1509-1564)

"The covenant of life is not preached equally to all, and among those to whom it is preached, does not always meet the same reception."

John Calvin was born in Noyon, France, in 1509. Unlike Luther, Calvin came from a solid middle-class background. Trained as a lawyer and as an authority on church canon law, Calvin wrote and taught for the educated. A full generation removed from Luther, Calvin was caught up in the reform spirit sweeping Europe. A thorough-going humanist, Calvin eventually angered the authorities and was forced to leave France in 1535. Calvin speaks of having undergone a sort of religious conversion in 1535 which made him an even more ardent advocate of reform.

Calvin spent two years essentially moving about to avoid the wrath of the Catholic Church. In 1536 he wrote his great treatise *The Institutes of Christian Religion*. This work seems to have almost immediately placed Calvin at the head of the Protestant movement in Europe at this time. He was brought to the attention of the authorities in Geneva, Switzerland, and was asked to take up residence there by a reformist by the name of Guillaume Farel. In 1538 Farel was expelled from Geneva and Calvin found himself in exile once again. In 1541 when Calvin was asked by the people of Geneva to return and take control of the Genevan Church, he immediately set about transforming Geneva into a theocracy, with strict rules of governance that often exceeded the strictures of the Catholic Church.

Calvin can be said to be the most influential of the Protestant Reformers, in that his ideas relating to predestination, the doctrine of the elect, and the doctrine of living saints, spread rapidly throughout Europe. Calvinists, by the end of the seventeenth century, substantially outnumbered the Lutheran factions within Protestant Europe.

(While Lutheranism came to dominate the early period of the Reformation, it was Calvinism that was to serve as the dynamic force of the Reformation in the latter part of the sixteenth century. John Calvin explained his Christian philosophy in his Institutes of the Christian Religion.*)*

Calvin's Institutes of the Christian Religion

The covenant of life is not preached equally to all, and among those to whom it is preached, does not always meet with the same reception. This diversity displays the unsearchable depth of the divine judgement, and is without doubt subordinate to God's purpose of eternal election. But if it is plainly owing to the mere pleasure of God that salvation is spontaneously offered to some, while others have no access to it, great and difficult questions immediately arise, questions which are inexplicable, when just views are not entertained concerning election and predestination....

By predestination we mean the eternal decree of God, by which he determined with himself whatever he wished to happen with regard to every man. All are not created on equal terms, but some are preordained to eternal life, others to eternal damnation; and, accordingly, as each has been created for one or other of these ends, we say that he has been predestinated to life or to death....

We say, then, that Scripture clearly proves this much, that God by his eternal and immutable counsel determined once for all those whom it was his pleasure one day to admit to salvation, and those whom, on the other hand, it was his pleasure to doom to destruction. We maintain that this counsel, as regards the elect, is founded on his free mercy, without any respect to human worth, while those whom he dooms to destruction are excluded from access to life by a just and blameless, but at the same time incomprehensible judgement. In regard to the elect, we regard calling as the evidence of election, and justification as another symbol of its manifestation, until it is fully accomplished by the attainment of glory. But as the Lord seals his elect by calling and justification, so by excluding the reprobate either from the knowledge of his name or the sanctification of his Spirit, he by these marks in a manner discloses the judgment which awaits them. I will here omit many of the fictions which foolish men have devised to overthrow predestination. There is no need of refuting objections which the moment they are produced abundantly betray their hollowness. I will dwell only on those points which either form the subject of dispute among the learned, or may occasion any difficulty to the simple, or may be employed by impiety as specious pretexts for assailing the justice of God.

(From Calvin's *Institutes of the Christian Religion*)

HENRY VIII OF ENGLAND

(1491-1547)

"That the King our sovereign lord, his heirs and successors, kings of this realm shall be taken, accepted and reputed the only supreme head in Earth of the Church of England called Anglicana Ecclesia."

Henry VIII was born in Greenwich Palace in London on June 28, 1491. Although his father, Henry VII, had been plagued by wars from both within and outside his kingdom, Henry was able to inherit a relatively peaceful realm. Henry's primary concerns were the solidification of his power and the need for revenue. He raised a great deal of money by increasing taxes and by confiscating the property of those who opposed his autocratic ways. Additionally, Henry was obsessed with producing a suitable male heir to the English throne. He had married his elder brother's widow, Catherine of Aragon, and wished to divorce her when she could not produce a male heir. When the pope refused to grant this divorce, Henry turned to his advisors and to Parliament to remedy the situation. This action would eventually lead to the break of the English crown with the Catholic Church. Ironic, since the pope had named Henry "Defender of the Faith" for having been so adamantly opposed to the Lutheran heresy. In 1534 Parliament approved *The Act of Supremacy*, establishing Henry as the head of The Church of England.

The events of 1534 did not make England a true Protestant country. Henry continued to hold to most of the tenets of the Catholic faith. Even after the passage of *The Six Articles* in 1539, which further spelled out the authority of the king over the English church, many of the orthodoxies of the Catholic Church remained imbedded in the Anglican Church. Over time, however, Protestant influences would infiltrate the Anglican system. Elizabeth I, Henry VIII's daughter, is credited with removing many of the Catholic traditions from the Anglican faith.

(The Act of Supremacy (1534) made King Henry VIII head of the Church of England, thus completing the break of England from the Catholic Church.)

The Act of Supremacy (1534)

The King's Grace to be Authorized Supreme Head.

1. Albeit the King's Majesty justly and rightfully is and ought to be the supreme head of the church of England and so is recognized by the clergy of this realm in their convocations, yet nevertheless for corroboration and confirmation thereof, and for increase of virtue in Christ's religion within this realm of England, and to repress and extirpate all errors, heresies, and other enormities and abuses heretofore used in the same: be it enacted by authority of this present parliament, That the King our sovereign lord, his heirs and successors, kings of this realm, shall be taken, accepted and reputed the only supreme head in earth of the church of England, called *Anglicana Ecclesia*;
2. and shall have and enjoy, annexed and united to the imperial crown of this realm, as well the title and style thereof, as all honors, dignities, pre-eminences, jurisdictions, privileges, authorities, immunities, profits and commodities to the said dignity of supreme head of the same church belonging and appertaining;
3. and that our said sovereign lord, his heirs and successors, kings of this realm, shall have full power and authority from time to time to visit, repress, redress, reform, order, correct, restrain and amend all such errors, heresies, abuses, offenses, contempts and enormities, whatsoever they be, which by any manner, spiritual authority, or jurisdiction ought or may lawfully be reformed, repressed, ordered, redressed, corrected, restrained or amended, most to the pleasure of Almighty God, the increase of virtue in Christ's religion, and for the conservation of the peace, unity and tranquility of this realm; and any usage, custom, foreign laws, foreign authority, prescription, or any other thing or things to the contrary hereof notwithstanding.

SIR THOMAS MORE

(1478-1535)

"They discuss no matter on the day that it is first brought forward."

Thomas More was born in London in 1478. He studied at the University of Oxford and took up the study of law after departing from Oxford. More earned a reputation as an excellent writer and was praised by fellow humanists as "the best of his countrymen." In 1499 More became a monk but seems to have tired of the restrictions of that life and entered politics as a member of Parliament in 1504. More briefly resigned from political life because of political differences with Henry VII, but became active again during the reign of Henry VIII. He was knighted in 1521 and became Speaker of the House of Commons in 1523. He was able to forge a close relationship with Henry VIII and was named Lord Chancellor in 1529. Despite his friendship with Henry VIII, More refused to recognize Henry's divorce from Catherine of Aragon and resigned the chancellorship in 1532. Henry's heart was hardened against More and he was eventually imprisoned and tried for treason. When More refused to take an oath swearing allegiance to the Anglican faith, he was sentenced to death and decapitated in 1535.

Thomas More is perhaps best remembered for his work *Utopia*. The title literally means nowhere. The work is ostensibly about a perfect society, but actually serves to promote More's philosophy relating to sixteenth century England. By describing life in Utopia he manages to critique the poverty, excessive wealth, and the political and religious abuses of the era. In addition, More makes a strong plea against war. The Utopians work together and share land and goods. They have only a six hour work day in order to insure time for relaxation and important pursuits of the mind. All righteous men are granted equal status. More's *Utopia* is one of the most important expressions of the humanist spirit during the Renaissance...

(Sir Thomas More was beheaded in 1535 for refusing to recognize Henry VIII's sovereignty over the English church. He is best remembered for his work Utopia, *published in 1516.)*

SIR THOMAS MORE'S *UTOPIA* (1516)

-Of The Island of Utopia and the Customs of its People

The Island of Utopia is shaped like a new moon, in breadth at the middle 200 miles, narrowing to the tips, which fetch about a compass of 500 miles, and are sundered by eleven miles, having in the space between them a high rock; so that that whole coast is a great haven, but the way into it is securely guarded by hidden rocks. It hath fifty-four large and fair cities, all built in one fashion and having like manners, institutions and laws. The chief and head is Amaurote, being the midmost. Every city hath an equal shire, with farms thereon; and of the husbandmen, half return each year to the city, their place being taken by a like number.

The city of Amaurote standeth four square, upon the River Anyder, and another lesser river floweth through it. The houses be fair and gorgeous, and the streets twenty foot broad; and at the back of each house a garden, whereby they set great store.

Each thirty families choose an officer, called a Siphogrant, and over every tenth siphogrant is a Tranibore. The prince and the tranibores hold council every third day, each day with two different siphogrants. They discuss no matter on the day that it is first brought forward. All the people are expert in husbandry, but each hath thereto his own proper craft of masonry or cloth-working, or some other; and, for the most part, that of his father. They work only six hours, which is enough—yea, and more for the store and abundance of things requisite, because all do work. There be none that are idle or busied about unprofitable occupations. In all that city and shire there be scarce 500 persons that be licensed from labour, that be neither too old nor too weak to work. Such be they that have license to learning in place of work. Out of which learned order be chosen ambassadors, priests, tranibores and the prince. For their clothing, they wear garments of skins for work, and woolen cloaks of one fashion and of the natural colour; and for the linen, they care only for the whiteness, and not the fineness; wherefore their apparel is of small cost.

The city consisteth of families; and for each family the law is there be not fewer than ten children, nor more than sixteen of about thirteen years. Which numbers they maintain by taking from one family and adding to another, or one city and another, or by their foreign cities which they have in the waste places of neighbour lands. The eldest citizen ruleth the family. In each quarter of the city is a market-place whither is brought the work of each family, and each taketh away that he needeth, without money or exchange.

To every thirty families there is a hall, whither cometh the whole siphogranty at the set hour of dinner or supper; and a nursery thereto. But in the country they dine and sup in their own houses. If any desire to visit another city, the prince giveth letters of licence. But wherever he goeth he must work the allotted task. All be partners, so that none may be poor or needy; and all the cities do send to the common council at Amaurote, so that what one lacketh another maketh good out of its abundance.

Their superfluities they exchange with other lands for what they themselves lack, which is little but iron; or for money, which they use but seldom, and that for the hiring of soldiers. Of gold and silver they make not rich vessels, but mean utensils, fetters and gyves; and jewels and precious stones they make toys for children.

Although there be not many that are appointed only to learning, yet all in childhood be instructed therein; and the more part do bestow in learning their spare hours. In the course of the stars and movings of the heavenly sphere they be expert, but for the deceitful divination thereof they never dreamed of it.

They dispute of the qualities of the soul and reason of virtue, and of pleasure, wherein they think the felicity of man to rest; they believe that the soul is immortal, and by the goodness of God ordained to felicity, and that to our virtues and good deeds rewards be appointed hereafter, and to evil deeds punishments. Which principles, if they were disannulled, there is no man but would diligently pursue pleasure by right or wrong. But now felicity resteth only in that pleasure that is good and honest. Virtue they define to be life according to nature, which prescribeth us a joyful life.

But of what they call counterfeit pleasures they make naught; as of pride in apparel and gems, or in vain honours; or of dicing; or hunting, which they deem the most abject kind of butchery. But of true pleasures they give to the soul intelligence and that pleasure that cometh of contemplation of the truth, and the pleasant remembrance of the good life past. Of pleasures of the body they count first those that be sensibly felt and perceived, and, thereto the body's health, which lacking, there is no place for any pleasure. But chiefest they hold the pleasures of the mind, the consciousness of virtue and the good life. Making little of the pleasures of appetite, they yet count it madness to reject the same for a vain shadow of virtue.

For bondmen, they have malefactors of their own people, criminals condemned to death in other lands, or poor labourers of other lands who, of their own free will, choose rather to be in bondage with them. The sick they tend with great affection; but, if the disease be not only incurable but full of anguish, the priests exhort them that they should willingly die, but cause him not to die against his will.

The women marry not before eighteen years, the men four years later. But if one have offended before marriage, he or she whether it be, is sharply punished. And before marriage the man and the woman are showed each to the other by discreet persons. To mock a man for his deformity is counted great reproach. They do not only fear their people from doing evil by punishments, but also allure them to virtue by rewards of honour. They have but few laws, reproving other nations that innumerable books of law and expositions upon the same be not sufficient. Furthermore, they banish all such as do craftily handle the laws, but think it meet that every man should plead his own matter.

-Of the Wars and the Religion of the Utopians

As touching leagues they never make one with any nation, putting no trust therein; seeing the more and holier ceremonies to league is knit up with, the sooner it is broken. Who perchance would change their minds if they lived here? But they be of opinion that no man should be counted an enemy who hath done no injury, and that the fellowship of nature is a strong league.

They count nothing so much against glory as glory gotten in war. And though they do daily practise themselves in the discipline of war, they go not to battle but in defence of their own country or their friends, or to right some assured wrong. They be ashamed to win the victory with much bloodshed, but rejoice if they vanquish their enemies by craft. They set a great price upon the life or person of the enemy's prince and of other chief adversaries, counting that they thereby save the lives of many of both parts that had otherwise been slain; and stir up neighbour peoples against them.

They lure soldiers out of all countries to do battle with them, and especially a savage and fierce people called the Zapoletes, giving them greater wages than any other nation will. But of their own people they thrust not forth to battle any against his will; yet if women be willing, they do in set field stand every one by her husband's side, and each man is compassed about by his own kinsfolks; and they be themselves stout and hardy and disdainful to be conquered. It is hard to say whether they be craftier in laying ambush or wittier in avoiding the same. Their weapons be arrows, and at handstrokes not swords but poleaxes; and engines of war they devise and invent wondrous wittily.

There be diverse kinds of religion. Some worship for God the sun, some the moon; some there be that give worship to a man that was once of the most excellent virtue; some believe that there is a certain godly power unknown, everlasting, incomprehensible; but all believe that there is one God, Maker and Ruler of the whole world. But after they heard us speak of Christ, with glad minds they agreed unto the same.

And this is one of their ancientest laws, that no man shall be blamed for reasoning in the maintenance of his own religion, giving to every man free liberty to believe what he would. Saving that none should conceive so base and vile an opinion as to think that souls do perish with the body, or that the world runneth at all adventures, governed by no divine providence.

They have priests of exceeding holiness, and therefore very few. Both childhood and youth are instructed of them, not more in learning than in good manners.

"This," quoth he, "is that order of the commonwealth which, in my judgement, is not only the best, but also that which alone of good right may claim and take upon it the name of a commonwealth or weal-publique."

Thus when Raphael had made an end of his tale, though many things came to mind, which in the manners and laws of that people seemed to be instituted and founded of no good reason; yet because I knew he was weary of talking, I said that we would choose another time to weigh and examine the same matters. But, in the meantime, I, Thomas More, as I cannot agree and consent to all things that he said, so must I needs confess and grant that many things be in the Utopian weal-publique which in our cities I may rather wish for than hope after.

(From an 18th century translation of Sir Thomas More's *Utopia*)

ULRICH ZWINGLI

(1484-1531)

"In the Gospel one learns that human doctrines and decrees do not aid in salvation."

Ulrich Zwingli was born in Wildhaus, Switzerland in 1484. Almost an exact contemporary of Luther (only a few weeks separates their birth), Zwingli was given an excellent education in philosophy and literature. Deeply moved by the reform movement started by Luther, Zwingli turned his attention to religious matters in his early twenties. He used Erasmus's version of the Greek New Testament and began to preach against the authority of the Church. He was in almost total agreement with Luther except on the issue of the Eucharist. Zwingli held the position that the Eucharist should be seen as merely symbolic of the body and blood of Christ.

Zwingli can be viewed as the father of the Protestant movement in Switzerland. His reform views were adopted in many of the metropolitan areas of Switzerland and paved the way for Calvin's entry into Geneva in 1538. His *Criticisms of the Catholic Church* forms the basis for the Swiss Protestant reform movement. Zwingli's reforms were not radical enough for certain zealous factions; he was killed in battle against the Anabaptists in 1531.

(In 1523, Ulrich Zwingli introduced a document in Zurich that clearly outlined the errors of the Catholic church.)

Zwingli Criticizes the Catholic Church

All who consider other teachings equal to or higher than the Gospel err, and they do not know what the Gospel is.

In the faith rests our salvation, and in unbelief our damnation; for all truth is clear in Christ.

In the Gospel one learns that human doctrines and decrees do not aid in salvation.

That Christ, having sacrificed himself once, is to eternity a certain and valid sacrifice for the sins of all faithful, wherefrom it follows that the Mass is not a sacrifice, but is a remembrance of the sacrifice and assurance of the salvation which Christ has given us.

That God desires to give us all things in his name, whence it follows that outside of this life we need no [intercession of the saints or any] mediator except himself.

That no Christian is bound to do those things which God has not decreed, therefore one may eat at all times all food, wherefrom one learns that the decree about cheese and butter [i.e., fasting from such foods at certain times of the year] is a Roman swindle.

That no special person can impose the ban upon [i.e., excommunicate] anyone, but the Church, that is, the congregation of those among whom the one to be banned dwells, together with their watchman, i.e., the pastor.

All that the so-called spiritual [i.e., the papal church] claims to have of power and protection belongs to the lay [i.e., the secular magistracy], if they wish to be Christians.

Greater offense I know not than that one does not allow priests to have wives, but permits them to hire prostitutes.

Christ has borne all our pains and labor. Hence whoever assigns to works of penance what belongs to Christ errs and slanders God.

The true divine Scriptures know naught about purgatory after this life.

The Scriptures know no priests except those who proclaim the word of God.

(From Ulrich Zwingli's *Selected Words* 1484-1531)

IGNATIUS OF LOYOLA

(1491-1556)

"We are to carry forward the message of the Church as soldiers of the Lord."

Ignatius Loyola was born in the Basque region of Spain in 1491. Of noble birth, he committed his life to that of a soldier and was seriously wounded in a battle against the French. While recovering from this painful injury, Loyola read a life of Jesus and a general history of the saints. From Loyola's own accounts we learn that he had a religious conversion and repudiated his previous decadent life. He began a particularly strenuous ascetic life and eventually went to the University of Paris to train himself in the teachings of the Church. In 1534 Loyola founded the Society of Jesus, better known as Jesuits.

Adopting the language of his former life as a soldier, Loyola created a militant organization. Nothing less than full commitment to the Catholic Church was accepted by the Jesuit order. *Loyola's Rules for the Jesuits* speaks to this strict code of discipline. In 1540 Pope Paul III formally recognized the Society of Jesus. The Society contained a force of some 1500 men at the time of Loyola's death in 1556. The Jesuits are credited with reestablishing the Catholic faith in many areas of Europe, as well as spreading the Church into other areas of the globe, most notably in North and South America. The other area of success for the Jesuits involved the spread of Catholic education. Numerous Jesuit missionaries founded educational institutions throughout the world, many of which are still in existence.

(The Counter-Reformation was an attempt to re-direct the Catholic church. The Jesuits, founded by Ignatius Loyola, followed a strict disciplinary code, refusing to compromise with the Protestants.)

Loyola's Rules for the Jesuits

In order to have the proper attitude of mind in the Church Militant we should observe the following rules:

1. Putting aside all private judgment, we should keep our minds prepared and ready to obey promptly and in all things the true spouse of Christ our Lord, our Holy Mother, the hierarchical Church.
2. To praise sacramental confession and the reception of the Most Holy Sacrament once a year, and much better once a month, and better still every week....
3. To praise the frequent hearing of Mass....
4. To praise highly the religious life, virginity, and continence; and also matrimony, but not as highly....
5. To praise the vows of religion, obedience, poverty, chastity, and other works of perfection and supererogation....
6. To praise the relics of the saints...[and] the stations, pilgrimages, indulgences, jubilees, Crusade indulgences, and the lighting of candles in the churches.
7. To praise the precepts concerning fasts and abstinences...and acts of penance....
8. To praise the adornments and buildings of churches as well as sacred images....
9. To praise all the precepts of the church....
10. To approve and praise the directions and recommendations of our superiors as well as their personal behaviour....
11. To praise both the positive and scholastic theology....
12. We must be on our guard against making comparisons between the living and those who have already gone to their reward, for it is no small error to say, for example: "This man knows more than St. Augustine'; 'He is another Saint Francis, or even greater.'...

13. If we wish to be sure that we are right in all things, we should always be ready to accept this principle: I will believe that the white that I see is black, if the hierarchical Church so defines it. For I believe that between...Christ our Lord and...His Church, there is but one spirit, which governs and directs us for the salvation of our souls.

(From *The Spiritual Exercises of St. Ignatius*)

HENRY IV, HENRY OF NAVARRE

(1553-1598)

"We ordain that the Catholic, Apostolic, and Roman religion shall be restored and reestablished in all places....."

Henry was born in 1553 in the region of Navarre in Southeastern France. Henry's family adopted the Huguenot faith (French Protestants). After the Peace of Augsburg in 1555, each of the German princes was allowed to choose between Lutheranism and Catholicism for their respective states. The religious wars that erupted in France, however, proved to be more difficult to solve. French Protestants were far outnumbered by the Catholic majority and were deeply resented by the Valois dynasty of France. The wars lasted off and on between 1562 and 1593. In 1572 it was arranged that Henry would marry Margaret, sister of King Charles IX. This marriage was hailed as advantageous to both Catholics and Protestants. Unfortunately, Catherine de Medici, regent for Charles IX, had arranged with certain Ultra-Catholic factions to murder Henry and other Huguenot leaders during the wedding celebration. The result was what became known as the Saint Bartholomew's Massacre when several thousand Huguenots were massacred throughout Paris. Henry, spared death by agreeing to swear an allegiance to the Catholic faith, spent nearly three years as a virtual prisoner in the Valois court. He eventually escaped and renounced his Catholic conversion in order to head up an opposition army.

When Henry III died in 1589, Henry found himself next in line to become King of France. His Protestant background made his claim to the crown tenuous at best. Rival claimants instigated war against Henry that lasted until 1593 when Henry agreed once again to adopt the Catholic faith. With the famous utterance, "Paris is worth a mass," Henry entered into Paris as the legitimate French king and set about improving the economy, which had been ravaged by the civil wars. He built roads, canals, and generally promoted commerce between the various sections of France. Perhaps his most important feat was to issue *The Edict of Nantes* in 1598. This edict recognized the Huguenots' right to worship freely and to maintain certain fortified cities within the French kingdom. Henry was generally well received by the people of France, but in 1598 he was stabbed to death by a Catholic fanatic in Paris.

(Religious conflicts continued throughout the sixteenth century. The French Calvinists, known as Huguenots, were heavily persecuted in France. On April 13, 1598, French King Henry IV recognized the Huguenot religion by issuing a document known as the Edict of Nantes.)

The Edict of Nantes

We have by this perpetual and irrevocable Edict pronounced, declared, and ordained and we pronounce, declare and ordain:

Art. I. Firstly, that the memory of everything done on both sides from the beginning of the month of March, 1585, until our accession to the Crown and during the other previous troubles, and at the outbreak of them, shall remain extinct and suppressed, as if it were something which had never occurred....

Art. II. We forbid all our subjects, of whatever rank and quality they may be, to renew the memory of these matters, to attack, be hostile to, injure or provoke each other in revenge for the past, whatever may be the reason and pretext...but let them restrain themselves and live peaceably together as brothers, friends, and fellow-citizens....

Art. III. We ordain that the Catholic, Apostolic, and Roman religion shall be restored and re-established in all places and districts of this our kingdom and the countries under our rule, where its practice has been interrupted....

Art. VI. And we permit those of the so-called Reformed religion to live and dwell in all the towns and districts of this our kingdom and the countries under our rule, without being annoyed, disturbed, molested or constrained to do anything against their conscience, or for this cause to be sought out in their houses and districts where they wish to live, provided that they conduct themselves in other respects to the provisions of our present Edict....

Art. XXI. Books dealing with the matters of the aforesaid so-called Reformed religion shall not be printed and sold publicly, except in the towns and districts where the public exercise of the said religion is allowed....

Art. XXII. We ordain that there shall be no difference or distinction, because of the aforesaid religion, in the reception of students to be instructed in Universities, Colleges, and schools, or of the sick and poor into hospitals, infirmaries, and public charitable institutions....

Art. XXVII. In order to reunite more effectively the wills of our subjects, as is our intention, and to remove all future complaints, we declare that all those who profess or shall profess, the aforesaid so-called Reformed religion are capable of holding and exercising all public positions, honours, offices, and duties whatsoever...in the towns of our kingdom...notwithstanding all contrary oaths.

(From the Edict of Nantes 1598)

PART TWO

(In the seventeenth century economic prosperity became entwined with the affairs of the state. The economic philosophy known as mercantilism stressed an excess of exports over imports {a favorable balance of trade}.)

Mercantilism

The ordinary means therefore to increase our wealth and treasure is by Forraign Trade wherein we must ever observe this rule; to sell more to strangers yearly than we consume of theirs in value. For suppose that when this Kingdom is plentifully served with the Cloth, Lead, Tinn, Iron, Fish and other native commodities, we doe yearly export the over-plus to forraign countries to the value of twenty two hundred thousand pounds; by which means we are enabled beyond the Seas to buy and bring in forraign wares for our use and Consumptions, to the value of twenty hundred thousand pounds; By this order duly kept in our trading, we may rest assured that the Kingdom shall be enriched yearly two hundred thousand pounds, which must be brought to us in so much Treasure; because that part of our stock which is not returned to us in wares must necessarily be brought home in treasure [i.e., gold or silver bullion].

(From Thomas Mun, *England's Treasure by Forraign Trade*)

JAMES I, KING OF ENGLAND

(1566-1625)

"Kings are also compared to fathers of families, for a king is truly parens patriae, the political father of his people."

James I of England, also known as James VI, King of Scotland, was born in Scotland in 1566. His mother, Mary Queen of Scots, a woman of strong Catholic convictions, was forced to abdicate her throne by Protestant factions in 1567. James was raised by staunch Protestant leaders and thus became embroiled in the debate between Protestant and Catholic rivals. James began his personal rule of Scotland in 1583 by escaping from the Protestant leaders who had held him as a virtual captive. Desiring the English crown, James entered into a direct alliance with Elizabeth I in 1586. Elizabeth, who died childless in 1603, provided in her will that James would ascend the throne. In 1603 he became James I of England and found himself embroiled in religious/political conflict once again. As King of England, he embraced High Anglicanism as a way to increase his royal power. Parliament at this time was increasingly influenced by a vocal faction known as the Puritans. The Puritans resented the decadent court life of James and his entourage and outwardly expressed their discontent. They also demanded a place for the Puritan faith within the Anglican Church. James, decidedly unsympathetic to the Puritan cause, took every opportunity to check their growing influence. Additionally, many Puritan groups were angered when the king authorized a new version of the Bible replete with updated language–what we refer to today as the King James Bible.

James was an advocate of the divine right of kings. In his work The Trew Law of Free Monarchy, James used biblical scripture to support the thesis that the king was God's agent on earth.

Much resentment was generated in Parliament when he insisted on reading entire segments of this work to the members during legislative sessions. Often these readings lasted for hours. By 1611, James had dismissed Parliament altogether, and ruled without Parliament until he needed it to support the German Protestants in 1621. By the time of his death in 1625, James had managed to alienate the Puritans and his Parliament. His son, who would rule as Charles I, would inherit these problems.
(In 1610, James I of England described the concept of divine right of Kings.)

James I on the Divine Rights of Kings

...The state of monarchy is the supremest thing upon earth, for kings are not only God's lieutenants upon earth and sit upon God's throne, but even by God himself are called gods...in the scriptures kings are called gods and so their power after a certain relation compared to the divine power. Kings are also compared to fathers of families, for a king is truly parens patriae, the politic father of his people. And lastly, kings are compared to the head of this microcosm of the body of man....

I conclude then this point touching the power of kings with this axiom of divinity, that as to dispute what God may do is blasphemy,...so is it sedition in subjects to dispute what a king may do in the height of his power. But just kings will ever be willing to declare what they will do, if they will not incur the curse of God. I will not be content that my power be disputed upon; but I shall ever be willing to make the reason appear of all my doings, and rule my actions according to my laws....I would wish you to be careful...that you do not meddle with the main points of government; that is my craft....It is an undutiful part in subjects to press their king wherein they know beforehand he will refuse them....
(From the writings of James I, 1610)

CHARLES I OF ENGLAND

(1600-1649)

"The King willeth that right be done according to the rights and customs of the land..."

Charles was born in Dunfermline, Scotland in 1600. He was the second son of James I but became first in line to the English throne upon the death of his elder brother. He took the throne upon his father's death in 1625. Like his father, Charles was a strong advocate of rule by divine right. He inherited a Parliament already aroused against the monarchy and proceeded to make things worse. His marriage to French princess Henrietta Maria angered the Protestant factions in England because of Henrietta's Roman Catholic background. Charles's foreign wars and the costly upkeep of his royal court caused him to ask Parliament for large sums of money. When Parliament balked, he often resorted to extra-parliamentary means to raise the necessary funds. Consequently, Charles convoked and dismissed numerous Parliaments during his reign.

In 1628 Parliament presented Charles with the Petition of Right. This document demanded Charles not tax without Parliament's consent, cease from arbitrary arrest of its members, and make general reforms within the royal government. Needing Parliament for his financial purposes, Charles agreed to the petition. Within a year (1629) Charles dismissed Parliament and went back to his old ways, ruling without a Parliament for the next eleven years. When the Scots rebelled against the Anglican Book of Common Prayer in 1640, Charles was forced to call back Parliament to raise money to put down the rebellion. This Parliament became known as the Short Parliament since it met for only one month after refusing the king's demands. Alas, Charles called Parliament back again in 1640. This Parliament became known as the Long Parliament; it met off and on until 1649. In 1642 Parliament and the king broke openly. The resulting civil war in England lasted for almost seven years. Charles was captured and eventually tried for treason. He was executed on January 27, 1649. After Charles's death the country was led by a member of the Puritan Army, one Oliver Cromwell.

(In many respects Charles I had inherited problems from previous kings. He, too, was an advocate of the divine right of kings. In 1628, Charles I was forced to accept the Petition of Right, which was aimed at limiting the king's power.)

The Parliament Petitions Charles I

[The Lords Spiritual and Temporal, and Commons in Parliament assembled] do humbly pray your Most Excellent Majesty, that no man hereafter be compelled to make or yield any gift, loan, benevolence, tax, or such like charge, without common consent by Act of Parliament; and that none be called to make answer, or take such oath, or give attendance, or be confined, or otherwise molested or disquieted concerning the same, or for refusal thereof; and that no freeman, in any such manner as is before-mentioned, be imprisoned or detained; and that your Majesty will be pleased to remove the said soldiers and mariners [who have been quartered in private homes], and that your people may not be so burdened in time to come; and that the foresaid commissions for proceeding by martial law, may be revoked and annulled; and that hereafter no commissions of like nature may issue forth to any person or persons whatsoever, to be executed as aforesaid, lest by colour of them any of your Majesty's subjects be destroyed or put to death, contrary to the laws and franchise of the land.

All which they most humbly pray of your Most Excellent Majesty, as their rights and liberties according to the laws and statutes of this realm.

[The Kings' reply: The King willeth that right be done according to the laws and customs of the realm; and that the statutes be put in due execution, that his subjects may have no cause to complain of any wrong or oppressions, contrary to their just rights and liberties, to the preservation whereof he holds himself as well obliged as of his prerogative.]

(From The Petition of Right, 1628)

OLIVER CROMWELL, LORD PROTECTOR

(1599-1658)

"So there is nothing he could have demanded that any of them would have denied him..."

Oliver Cromwell was born in Huntington, England, in 1599. His family at the time of his birth were minor landowners, but through an advantageous marriage and a substantial inheritance from an uncle, Cromwell was a wealthy man. Cromwell's early economic struggles seem to have led to his conversion to the Puritan faith. Through his Puritan friends Cromwell became associated with politics. Most of his political connections were disenchanted with Charles I and considered his rule of England too arbitrary. Additionally, the Puritans questioned Charles's Roman Catholic ties. When Charles convened Parliament in 1640 to challenge the Scottish rebels, Cromwell entered Parliament.

Cromwell found himself among like-minded men while in Parliament. The Puritan faction had grown more vocal against the king, and when the open break between king and Parliament occurred in 1642, Cromwell volunteered his services to the Parliamentary army. Cromwell quickly earned a reputation as a competent leader of men. By 1645 he was at the head of the New Model Army and was the key factor in the army's defeat of the king's army at Naseby in 1645. By 1647 the Parliamentary forces were in control of the country. Cromwell sought to return to civilian life, but strife between the army and Parliament prevented him from doing so. In time Cromwell sided with the military and by so doing kept the country from sliding into chaos once again. Eventually elevated to the role of Supreme Commander of the Parliamentary Army, Cromwell conducted vicious campaigns against the Irish and led the army against the rebellious Scots. These military forays cemented Cromwell's reputation, and when he defeated forces led by Charles II in 1651, he was widely hailed as "the savior of the Commonwealth".

In 1653 Cromwell was given the title of Lord Protector and ruled under this title until his death in 1658. Cromwell, while advocating a degree of religious toleration, imposed strict Puritan rules on the people of England. Theaters were shut down and a strict moral code was imposed. While he did have some success in the area of foreign policy, his rule became very unpopular. When the Stuart dynasty was restored under Charles II in 1660, Cromwell's body was disinterred and hanged in effigy. Cromwell's legacy is still a matter of great debate in English history.

(The English Civil War, 1642 to 1649, eventually brought Oliver Cromwell to power in England. Cromwell was both praised and reviled in England.)

Description of Oliver Cromwell by the Earl of Clarendon

He was one of those men whom his enemies cannot condemn without at the same time also praising. For he could never have done half that mischief without great parts of courage and industry and judgment. And he must have had a wonderful understanding of the natures and humours of men and a great dexterity in applying them...[to] raise himself to such a height....

When he first appeared in Parliament, he seemed to have a person in no degree gracious, no ornament of discourse, none of those talents which reconcile the affections of the standers-by; yet as he grew into his place and authority, his parts seemed to be renewed, as if he concealed faculties til he had occasion to use them....

After he was confirmed and invested Protector...he consulted with very few...nor communicated any enterprise he resolved upon with more than those who were to have principal parts in the execution of it; nor to them sooner than was absolutely necessary. What he once resolved...he would not be dissuaded from, nor endure any contradiction....

In all other matters which did not concern...his jurisdiction, he seemed to have great reverence for the law.... And as he proceeded with...indignation and haughtiness with those who were refractory and dared to contend with his greatness, so towards those who complied with his good pleasure, and courted his protection, he used a wonderful civility, generosity, and bounty.

To reduce three nations [England, Ireland, and Scotland], which perfectly hated him, to an entire obedience to all his dictates; to awe and govern those nations by an army that was not devoted to him and wished his ruin; this was an instance of a very prodigious address. But his greatness at home was but a shadow of the glory he had abroad. It was hard to discover which feared him most, France, Spain, or the Netherlands.... As they did all sacrifice their honour and their interest to his pleasure, so there is nothing he could have demanded that any of them would have denied him. (From the writings of the Earl of Clarendon)

Charles I was convicted of Treason and was beheaded on January 30, 1649.)

The Execution of Charles I (1649)

To the executioner he said, iI shall say but very short prayers, and when I thrust out my hands–"

Then he called to the bishop for his cap, and having put it on, asked the executioner, "Does my hair trouble you?" And the executioner desired him to put it under his cap, which as he was doing by help of the bishop and the executioner, he turned to the bishop and said, "I have a good cause, and a gracious God on my side."

The bishop said, "There is but one stage more, which, though turbulent and troublesome, yet is a very short one.... It will carry you from earth to heaven...to a crown of glory...."

Then the king asked the executioner, "Is my hair well?"

And taking off his cloak and George [the Order of the Garter, bearing a figure of Saint George], he delivered his George to the bishop....

Then putting off his doublet and being in his waistcoat, he put on his cloak again, and looking upon the block, said to the executioner, "You must set it fast."

The executioner. "It is fast, sir."

King. "It might have been a little higher."

Executioner. "It can be no higher, sir."

King. "When I put out my hands this way, then–"

Then having said a few words to himself, as he stood with hands and eyes lifted up, immediately stooping down he laid his neck upon the block; and the executioner, again putting his hair under his cap, his Majesty, thinking he had been going to strike, bade him, "Stay for the sign."

Executioner. "Yes, I will, as it please your Majesty."

After a very short pause, his Majesty stretching forth his hands, the executioner at one blow severed his head from his body; which being held up and showed to the people, was with his body put into a coffin covered with black velvet and carried into his lodging.

His blood was taken up by diverse persons for different ends; by some as trophies of the villainy; by others as relics of a martyr. (James Harvey Robinson (Ed.), Readings in European History, Vol 2, Boston Ginn & Co, 1906)

THOMAS HOBBES

(1588-1679)

"So men invade each other, first for gain, second for safety, and third for reputation."

Thomas Hobbes came of age in one of the most turbulent periods in English history. He would live to see the execution of King Charles I in 1649, the rule of Oliver Cromwell, and eventually the restoration of the Stuart monarchy in Charles II (1660). Consequently, Hobbes developed a secular view of history. His chief aim was to provide a justification for the political state. Amid the chaos of his time, he advocated rule by an absolute sovereign. In Hobbes's view, only a state ruled by an absolute power could bring order to England.

Hobbes's Leviathan, written in 1651, is his best known work. The title itself gives direct insight into the type of political state advocated by Hobbes. Leviathan is drawn from the *Old Testament* and refers to a great sea monster. Hobbes intended for his absolute government to be a sort of all-controlling monster. He weighs against democracy as being too cumbersome and inadequate to control the basic desires of mankind. Only an absolute ruler with complete authority could rein in the greed and lust of the people. It is important to note that Hobbes does not necessarily favor a monarchy over other types of dictatorial rule. By sovereign he refers to any ruler who maintains law and order. His sovereign may be a king or a dictator such as Oliver Cromwell.

Another important aspect of Hobbes's *Leviathan* is his espousal of the social contract. The social contract, as described by Hobbes, represents the agreement between the people and the absolute ruler. The people give up a large measure of personal liberty in exchange for order and protection. Hobbes viewed the social contract as inviolable as long as life and property are defended by the absolute ruler.

Hobbes's *Leviathan* stands with Machiavelli's *The Prince* as one of the most important political treatises of the early modern period. He would inspire such thinkers as John Locke, Montesquieu, and Jean Jacques Rousseau to develop their own versions of the social contract.

LEVIATHAN
THOMAS HOBBES

I-Of Man

Nature, the art whereby God hath made and governs the world, is by the art of man so imitated that he can make an artificial animal. For by art is created that great leviathan called a commonwealth or state, which is but an artificial man; in which the sovereignty is an artificial soul, as giving life and motion; the magistrates and other officers the joints; reward and punishment the nerves; concord, health; discord, sickness; lastly, the pacts or covenants by which the parts were first set together resemble the 'fiat' of God at the Creation.

To describe this artificial man, I will consider: First, the matter and the artificer, both which is man; secondly, how it is made; thirdly, what is a Christian commonwealth; lastly, what is the kingdom of darkness.

And first, of man. The thoughts of man are, singly, every one a representation of some quality or accident of a body without us, called an object. There is no conception in the mind which has not first been begotten upon the organs of sense. The cause of sense is the eternal object which presseth upon the proper organ; not that, as hath been taught in the schools, the thing 'sendeth forth a visible or audible species.'

Imagination is the continuity of an image after the object is removed. When we would express that the image is decaying, we call it memory; in sleep, we call it dreams.

Of all invention, the most notable is that of speech, names, the register of thoughts; which are notes for remembrance, or signs, for transference. Truth consisteth in the right ordering of names in our affirmations. Words are wise men's counters, but the money of fools.

Reasoning is the reckoning, the addition and subtraction of the sequences of words, the sum being the conclusion. Which conclusions may be absurd, because men do not start–except in geometry–from the definitions of the words. Reason, therefore, implies speech.

In animals there are two sorts of motions–vital and voluntary. The beginnings of motion within man are called 'endeavour.' Appetite is a motion towards; aversion is a motion fromwards. Some are born in us, some are products of experience. The object of a man's appetite he calls "good"; of his aversion, "evil"; whether in promise (beautiful and ugly), in effect (pleasant, painful), or as means (useful, hurtful). Pleasures and pains arise from an object present, of the senses; or in expectation, of the mind. Thus 'pity' is the imagining of a like calamity befalling oneself.

'Deliberation' is the sum of the successive appetites or aversions which are concluded by the doing or not doing of the particular thing. 'Will' is the last appetite in deliberating. So, in the enquiry of the truth, opinions correspond to appetites, and the final judgement, the last opinion, to the will.

There are two kinds of knowledge; of "fact" and of "the consequence of one affirmation to another." The former is nothing else but sense and memory, and is absolute; the latter is called science, and is conditional. The register of the first is called history, natural or civil; that of the second is contained in books of philosophy, in corresponding groups–natural philosophy, and civil philosophy or politics. Natural philosophy breaks up into a number of groups, including mental and moral science.

Power is present means, whencesoever derived, to attain some future apparent good. Value is the price that will be given for the use of a man's power. To honour a man is to acknowledge his power; to dishonour him is to depreciate it. The public worth of a man is the value set on him by the commonwealth.

By manners, I mean those qualities of mankind which are concerned with their living together in peace and unity. Desire of power tends to produce strife; other desires, as for ease, or for knowledge, incline men to obey a common power. To receive benefits, or to do injuries, greater than can be repaid or expiated, tends to make us hate the benefactor or the injured party.

II-Of Contract and Sovereignty

Nature hath made men so equal, in the faculties of body and mind that are born in them, that one man cannot in respect of these claim to himself any benefit to which another may not pretend. From this equality ariseth equality of hope in the attaining of our ends. Therefore, if two men desire the same thing which they cannot both enjoy they become enemies, and seek each the destruction of the other, each mistrusting the other. So men invade each other, first for gain, second for safety, and third for reputation.

Hence, while men live without a common power to keep them all in awe, they are in a state of war, every man against every man. In this state, notions of right and wrong, justice and injustice, have no place. Probably there never was actually such an universal condition; but we see it now among savage races and in the mutual relations of sovereigns. In this state of war, reason suggesteth articles of peace upon which men may agree; which articles are otherwise called the laws of nature.

The right "of nature" is the right of self-preservation. "Liberty" is the absence of impediments to the exercise of power. A "law of nature" is a precept of reason forbidding a man to do what is destructive of his own life. In the state of nature every man has a "right" to everything. Thus security comes only of the first fundamental law: "To seek peace and follow it," and "by all means we can defend ourselves."

The second law follows: "To lay down the right to everything, claiming only so much against others as we concede to others against ourselves." This right being renounced or transferred, injustice is the revocation of that act. But since the object of a voluntary act is good to oneself, such renunciation is not valid if not good for oneself; hence a man cannot renounce the right of self-preservation.

The transferring of right, if not mutual, is free gift; if mutual, it is contract. When this is not simultaneous there is a covenant or pact. The covenant can become void only through some new fact arising after it was made. A covenant not to defend oneself against force by force is void *per se*.

The third law is: "That men perform their covenant, made," without which covenants are vain, and the state of war continues. The definition of injustice is "the not-performance of a covenant." No covenant is valid until there exists some power that can enforce the performance of it by penalties; that is, until there is a commonwealth. What is done to a man conformable to his own will signified to the doer is no injury to him.

The fourth law is that of "gratitude"; that a man receiving a free gift endeavour that the giver may not suffer thereby. A fifth is "conplaisance"–that every man strive to accommodate himself to the rest. Others are pardon on repentance, and nonvindictiveness of punishment; and the common enjoyment–or, failing that, distribution by lot–of what cannot be equally divided.

Persons are either natural and actual, or fictitious and artificial, i.e., representing someone else, or even something else: as a church, a hospital, a bridge. When the representative has authority from the represented, we call the former the 'actor,' and the latter the 'author.' One person may artificially represent a multitude.

Now, men being in the state of nature may agree together; but there is no security, unless there be a power to enforce the covenant. Such a power can be created only if they agree together to confer all their own power on one man or one assembly; so that all the acts of such person or assembly have authority as from each one of them, and each one of them submits his individual will to that of such person or assembly. The multitude so united in one person is a commonwealth. This is the generation of that leviathan or mortal god to which, under the Immortal God, we owe our peace and defence.

He that carrieth this person is called "sovereign," and everyone beside is his "subject." This sovereign power may be attained either by natural force, "acquisition," or by voluntary "institution."

They that have instituted a commonwealth by covenant cannot make a new covenant contrary thereto without permission of the sovereign, since this is a breaking of their covenant with each other. On his part there is no covenant, so that breach of covenant by him cannot be pleaded as warranting abrogation of the covenant made. The sovereign cannot do the subjects injustice because, since he has their authority, what he does to them is done by their own will; so also they cannot punish him.

Since the sovereign was instituted for peace and defence, he controls the means to war and peace, and judges of opinions as conducing to peace or endangering it. He prescribes the rules of property, since in the state of nature there is no property; he has the right of adjudicature; of making war and peace with other commonwealths; of choosing all counsellors in peace and war; of rewarding and punishing, according to the law he has made and of bestowing honour. Nay, if he grants away any of these powers the grant is null.

The sovereignty may be in one man, or in a limited assembly, or in an assembly of all–monarchy, aristocracy, democracy; these three forms only, though when they are misliked they are called other names. In any case, the power of the sovereign is absolute, whether a monarch or an assembly. He is the representative of the commonwealth, not deputies who may be chosen to tender positions.

The three forms differ not in the power of the sovereign, but in their advantageousness. In monarchy, the private interest of the sovereign must coincide with that of the commonwealth as a whole; much more so than in aristocracy or democracy. An assembly cannot receive counsel secretly; a monarchy has the benefit of a single will instead of conflicting wills. There is no government by the mixture of the types, e.g., an elective "king" is not a sovereign, but a minister.

Men submit themselves to an instituted sovereign, for fear of each other; to an acquired sovereignty, for fear of the sovereign. Acquired sovereignty or dominion is either by generation (paternal) or by conquest. A family, however, does not amount to a commonwealth, unless it be so great that it may not be subdued by war. Acquired sovereignty is absolute for the same reasons as instituted sovereignty.

III-The Natural Commonwealth

Liberty is absence of impediments to motion. It is consistent with fear, also with necessity; for a voluntary act is yet necessary as having a cause which is a link in a chain of causes up to the First Cause, which is God. But men have created artificial impediments or bonds called laws. The liberty of the subject lies only in such things as the sovereign has permitted, for he hath power to regulate all, even life and death, at his own will. The liberty praised in Rome and Athens was the liberty of the commonwealth as against other commonwealths.

The subject has liberty to disobey the sovereign's command if it contravene the law that the right of self-preservation cannot be abrogated, unless it be to endanger himself for the preservation of the commonwealth, as with soldiers. The subjects' obligation of obedience lasts so long as the sovereign's power of defending them, that being the purpose of his being made sovereign.

By systems I mean numbers of men joined in one interest. These are political, constituted by law; and private, permitted or forbidden by law. All, except a commonwealth, are subordinate to the commonwealth, and have not the character of sovereignty. The rights of governing bodies are only those expressly conceded by law, either generally or to them specifically. Systems in the commonwealth correspond to muscles in the natural body.

The nourishment of the commonwealth is its commodities or products, the distribution of which must be at the will of the sovereign, whether of land or of commodities, exchanged internally or trafficked abroad.

The procreation, or children, of a commonwealth are its "plantations," or "colonies," which may be commonwealths themselves, as children emancipated, or remain parts of the commonwealth.

By civil laws I mean those laws that men are bound to obey as members of any commonwealth. The sovereign is the sole legislator, and is not subject to the laws which he can repeal at pleasure. The civil laws are the laws of nature expressed as commands of the commonwealth, or the will of the sovereign so expressed; whatever is not the law of nature must be expressly made known and published. Both the law of nature and written law require interpretation, which is by sentence of the judge constituted by sovereign authority.

An intention of breaking the law is a sin; issuing in a breach of the law it is crime. Violation of the laws of nature is always and everywhere sin; it is crime only when a violation of the laws of a commonwealth. Unavoidable ignorance of a law is a complete excuse for breaking it, but ignorance due to lack of diligence is not unavoidable. Terror of present death, or the order of the sovereign, is a complete excuse. And many circumstances may serve as extenuation.

A punishment is an evil inflicted by public authority on him that hath done or omitted that which is said to be by the same authority a transgression of the law, to the end that the will of men may thereby be the better disposed to obedience. Now, this right of punishment is not transferred by the subjects to the sovereign, since they cannot surrender their right of self-defence against violence. But as all before had the natural right of hurting others, that right is left by the covenant to the sovereign alone, strengthened by the resignation thereof by the rest.

Punishments inflicted by man are "corporal" or "pecuniary," or "ignominy," or "imprisonment," or "exile," or mixed of these. Corporal are capital, with or without torment, and less than capital. Pecuniary includes deprivation not only of money but also of lands or other saleable goods; but such deprivation, if it is by way of compensation to the person injured, is not really punishment. Imprisonment, when it is only for the custody of a person accused, is not punishment. Exile is not so much a punishment as a command or permission to escape punishment, except when accompanied by deprivation of goods.

Infirmities of a commonwealth arise–from the first institution, when the sovereign has not assumed sufficient power; from such doctrines as that each man privately is the judge of good or evil actions, or sins if he obey the commonwealth against his "conscience"; that the sovereign is subject to the civil laws; that private property excludes sovereign rights; that sovereign power may be divided, which is the worst of all; and from other causes, as of money grudged for wars; monopolies, over-potent subjects or corporation, insatiable desire of dominion. But when a country is conquered, that is the dissolution of the commonwealth.

Of the sovereign's duties the first is to surrender none of his powers, and the second to see that they be known, to which end, and the understanding of it, the people must be rightly instructed.

Further, that he administer justice equally to all people, and impose equal taxes, and make good laws (I say good, not just, since no law can be unjust), and choose good counsellors.

Subjects owe simple obedience to the sovereign in all things whatsover, except what is contrary to the laws of God. Therefore, it remains here to speak of the kingdom of God, Whose subjects are they that believe in Him. God declareth His laws either by natural reason, or by revelation, or by the voice of prophets. He is necessarily sovereign, for the one reason that He is omnipotent.

IV-Of A Christian Commonwealth

Of God speaking by the voice of a prophet are two signs: that the prophet worketh miracles, and that he teacheth no other religion than that established. These two must go together. And since miracles have ceased, it is clear that God no longer speaks by prophets.

But He hath revealed Himself in Scripture–that is, in those books which are in the canon ordained. But whether their authority be derived from the civil sovereignty or is of a universal church to which all sovereigns are subordinate is another question. It may be seen, however, from Scripture that the kingdom of God therein spoken of is a civil kingdom, which is that kingdom of God by Christ which was interrupted by the revolt of the Israelites and the election of Saul.

A church is a term used in many senses, but in one only can it be treated as a person having power to will, command, or do any action whatever. And according to this sense I define a church to be 'a company of men professing Christian religion, united in the person of one sovereign at whose command they ought to assemble, and without whose authority they ought not to assemble.' It follows that a church that is assembled in any commonwealth that hath forbidden them to assemble is an unlawful assembly.

There are Christians in the dominions of several princes and states; but every one of them is subject to that commonwealth of which he is himself a member, and consequently cannot be subject to the commands of any other person. There is therefore no such universal church as all are bound to obey.

The original covenant with Abraham gave him the sole right, which is the inheritance of every sovereign, to punish any subject who should pretend to a private vision for the countenancing of any doctrine which Abraham should forbid. This covenant established that kingdom of God which was interrupted by the secular kingdom of Saul. The coming of Christ was to restore that kingdom by a new covenant; which kingdom was to be in another world after the Resurrection. The power ecclesiastical was left by Him to the apostles, but manifestly not a coercive power on earth, as Christ's own power on earth was not.

Christ, therefore, by His coming did not withdraw any of the power from civil sovereigns, and if they do commit the government of their subjects in matter of religion to the Pope, he holdeth that charge not as being above the civil sovereign, but by his authority.

But as for disagreement between the laws of God and the civil laws of the sovereign, the laws of God, which must in no wise be disobeyed, are those which are necessary to salvation; and these are summed up in the will to obey the law of God and the belief that Jesus is the Christ. But the private man may not set up to judge whether the ordinance of the sovereign be against the law of God or whether the doctrine which he imposeth consist with the belief that Jesus is the Christ.

But in the Scripture there is mention also of another power, the kingdom of Satan, 'the prince of the powers of the air,' which is a confederacy of deceivers that, 'to obtain dominion over men in this present world, endeavours by dark and erroneous doctrines to extinguish in them the light both of nature and of the Gospel, and so to dis-prepare them for the kingdom of God to come.'

And such darkness is wrought first by abusing the light of the Scriptures so that we know them not; secondly by introducing the demonology of the heathen poets; thirdly, by mixing with the Scripture divers relics of the religion and much of the erroneous philosophy of the Greeks; and, fourthly, by mingling with these false or uncertain traditions and feigned or uncertain history.

WILLIAM III (1650-1702) AND MARY II (1662-1694) OF ENGLAND

(RULED 1689-1702)

"That the pretended power of suspending laws, or the execution of laws, by regal authority, without consent of Parliament is illegal."

William, also known as William of Orange, was born in Holland in 1650. Mary, daughter of James II of England, was born in 1662. William and Mary were first cousins, as both were the grandchildren of Charles I of England. Charles II of England arranged a marriage between the two in order to promote an alliance between England and Holland. From all accounts, Mary was not thrilled with the marriage; William, twelve years older, was indifferent. Over time the relationship seems to have grown into one of mutual respect.

The rule of James II was a tumultuous one. Members of Parliament resented his attempts to bypass them and were deeply suspicious of James's Catholic leanings. Parliament and James II came into direct conflict when he announced in 1688 that his son would be baptized into the Roman Catholic faith. William and Mary were invited by Parliament to take the crown from the Catholic upstart. This was a logical choice in that William was able to bring a substantial army to England to make his claim to the crown. When William landed in England in 1688, he received a warm welcome, particularly from English landowners who identified their interests with the Protestant faction. James, choosing not to fight, fled to France and permanent exile. The reign of William and Mary lasted from 1689 until William's death in 1702. (Mary died of smallpox in 1694.)

William and Mary agreed to sign *The English Bill of Rights* as a condition for taking the crown. *The Bill of Rights* places direct limits on the power of the English monarchy. It essentially outlines what the monarchy cannot do. After the signing of this bill of rights, England can be said to have operated as a true Constitutional Monarchy. The events that brought William and Mary to power were essentially bloodless, thereby earning this period of English history the name The Glorious Revolution.

(Upon Oliver Cromwell's death, England once again was subjected to political instability. The English civil war had not solved all the issues between King and Parliament. When William and Mary ascended to the throne in 1689, stability was at long last obtained. William and Mary signed a Bill of Rights in 1689.)

The English Bill of Rights (1689)

...And thereupon the said lords spiritual and temporal, and commons,...pursuant to their respective letters and elections, being now assembled in a full and free representation of this nation, taking into their most serious consideration the best means for attaining the ends aforesaid, do in the first place (as their ancestors in like case have usually done), for the vindicating and asserting their ancient rights and liberties, declare:

1. That the pretended power of suspending laws, or the execution of laws, by regal authority, without consent of parliament, is illegal.
2. That the pretended power of dispensing with laws, or the execution of laws, by regal authority, as it has been assumed and exercised of late, is illegal.
3. That levying money for or to the use of the crown by pretense of prerogative, without grant of parliament, for longer time or in other manner, that the same is or shall be granted, is illegal.
4. That it is the right of subjects to petition the king, and all commitments and prosecutions for such petitioning are illegal.
5. That the raising or keeping a standing army within the kingdom in time of peace, unless it be with consent of parliament, is against law.
6. That the subjects who are Protestants may have arms for their defense suitable to their conditions, and as allowed by law.
7. That election of members of parliament ought to be free.
8. That the freedom of speech, and debates of proceedings in parliament, ought not to be impeached or questioned in any court or place out of parliament.
9. That excessive bail ought not to be required, nor excessive fines imposed, nor cruel and unusual punishments inflicted.

10. That jurors ought to be full impaneled and returned, and jurors which pass upon men in trials for high treason ought to be freeholders.
11. That all grants and promises of fines and forfeitures of particular persons before conviction are illegal and void.
12. And that for redress of all grievances, and for the amending, strengthening, and preserving of the laws, parliament ought to be held frequently.

And they do claim, demand, and insist upon all and singular premises, as their undoubted rights and liberties; and that no declarations, judgments, doings, or proceedings, to the prejudice of the people in any of the said premises, ought in any wise to be drawn hereafter into consequence or example.

To which demand of their rights they are particularly encouraged by the declaration of his Highness the prince of Orange as being the only means for obtaining a full redress and remedy therein.
(From The English Bill of Rights, 1689)

JOHN LOCKE

(1632-1704)

"Perception, then, is the first operation of intellectual faculties, and the inlet of all knowledge into our minds."

John Locke was born in England in 1632. Noted not just as a philosopher, but as an Oxford Don, scientist, medical doctor, and economist, he is truly one of the most eclectic thinkers in the Western tradition. Locke, in direct contrast to Thomas Hobbes, believed in the essential goodness of man. According to Locke, it is society that corrupts man. In advocating certain inalienable rights inherent to all men, Locke would influence the budding Constitutional Monarchy in England and eventually the revolutionary movements in America and France.

Locke's *An Essay Concerning Human Understanding* attempts to determine the limits of what mankind can know. Locke felt that man enters the world as a blank slate, what he referred to as a tabula rasa. This empirical view of philosophy holds that we have no knowledge prior to experience. We can know only the appearances and not the underlying qualities that produce these experiences.

An Essay Concerning Human Understanding stands as a cornerstone of empirical philosophy. To a large extent the direction of empirical philosophy was in response to Locke's essay. Berkeley, Hume, and eventually Kant, all make direct references to Locke in their attempts to address the notion of the limits of human understanding.

AN ESSAY CONCERNING HUMAN UNDERSTANDING
JOHN LOCKE

I-The Nature of Simple Ideas

"Idea" being that term which, I think, serves best to stand for whatsoever is the object of the understanding, I have used it to express whatever is meant by phantasm, notion, species, or whatever it is the mind can be employed about in thinking. Let us, then, suppose the mind to be, as we say, white paper void of all characters–without any ideas. Whence comes it by that vast store which the busy and boundless fancy of man has painted on it with an almost endless variety? To this, I answer in one word–experience; in that all our knowledge is founded, and from that it ultimately derives itself.

Let anyone examine his own thoughts and thoroughly search his understanding, and then let him tell me whether of all the original ideas he has there are any other than of the objects of his senses, or of the observations of his mind considered as objects of his reflection.

Though the qualities that affect our senses are, in the things themselves, so united and blended that there is no separation, no distance between them, yet it is plain the ideas they produce in the mind enter by the senses simple and unmixed. For though the sight and touch often take in from the same object at the same time different ideas, yet the simple ideas thus united in the same subject are as perfectly distinct as those that come in by different senses; the coldness and hardness which a man feels in a piece of ice being as distinct ideas in the mind as the smell and whiteness of a lily, and each of them being in itself uncompounded contains nothing but one uniform appearance, or conception, in the mind, and is not distinguishable into different ideas.

When the understanding is once stored with these simple ideas, it has the power to repeat, compare and unite them even to an almost infinite variety, and so can make at will new complex ideas. But it is not in the power of any most exalted wit or enlarged understanding, by any quickness or variety of thought, to invent or frame one new simple idea in the mind, nor to destroy those that are there. I would have anyone try to fancy any taste which had never affected his palate, or frame the idea of a scent he had never smelt; and when he can do this, I will also conclude that a blind man hath ideas of colours and a deaf man true, distinct notions of sound.

There are some ideas which have admittance only through one sense which is peculiarly adapted to receive them. Thus, light and colours come in only by the eye, all kinds of noises by the ear, the tastes and smells by the nose and palate. The most considerable of those belonging to the touch are heat, cold and solidity–which is the idea that belongs to the body, whereby we conceive it to fill space.

Simple ideas of divers senses are the ideas of space or extension, figure, rest and motion, for these make perceivable impressions on the eyes and touch, and we can receive and convey into our minds the ideas of the extension, figure, motion and rest of bodies by seeing and feeling.

The mind, receiving the ideas mentioned in the foregoing from without, when it turns its view inward upon itself and observes its own actions about those ideas it has, takes from thence other ideas which are as capable to be the objects of its contemplation as any of those it received from foreign things.

The two great and principal actions of the mind which are most frequently considered, and which are so frequent that everyone that pleases may take notice of them in himself, are these two: perception or thinking, and volition or will. The power of thinking is called the understanding, and the power of volition is called the will. And these two powers or abilities in the mind are denominated faculties. Modes of these simple ideas of reflection are rememberance, discerning, reasoning, judging, knowledge, faith.

It has, further, pleased our wise Creator to annes to several objects and to the ideas which we received from them, as also to several of our thoughts, a concomitant pleassure, and that in several objects to several degrees, that those faculties which He has endowed us with might not remain wholly unemployed by us. Pain has the same efficacy and use to set us on work that pleasure we being as ready to employ our faculties to avoid that as to pursue this. Existence and unity are two other ideas that are suggested to the understanding by every object without and every idea within.

Nor let anyone think these too narrow bounds for the capacious mind of man to expatiate in, which takes its flight farther than the stars and cannot be confined by the limits of the world, that extends its thoughts often even beyond the utmost expansion of matter and makes excursions into that incomprehensible inane.

Nor will it be so strange to think these few simple ideas sufficient to employ the quickest thought or largest capacity if we consider how many words may be made out of the various composition of twenty-four letters; or if, going one step farther, we will but reflect on the variety of combinations that may be made with barely one of the above mentioned ideas–viz. number, whose stock is inexhaustible. And what a large and immense field doth extension alone afford the mathematicians!

II-Of Idea-Producing Qualities

The power to produce any idea in our mind I call quality of the subject wherein the power is. Qualities are, first, such as are utterly inseparable from the body in what state soever it be. These I call original or primary qualities, which I think we may observe to produce simple ideas in us–viz. solidity, extension, figure, motion or rest, and number.

Secondly, such qualities which in truth are nothing in the objects themselves, but powers to produce various sensations in us by their primary qualities–i.e. by the bulk, figure, texture and motion of their insensible parts. These secondary qualities are colours, sounds, tastes, etc. From whence it is easy to draw this observation: that the ideas of primary qualities of bodies are resemblances of them, but the ideas produced in us by the secondary qualities have no resemblance in them at all.

If anyone will consider that the same fire that at one distance produces in us the sensation of warmth does, at a nearer approach, produce in us the far different sensation of pain, let him bethink himself what reason he has to say that this idea of warmth, which was produced in him by the fire, is actually in the fire; and his idea of pain, which the same fire produced in him in the same way, is not in the fire. The particular bulk, number, figure and motion of the parts of fire or snow are really in them, whether anyone's senses perceive them or not; and, therefore, they may be called real qualities, because they really exist in those bodies. But light, heat, whiteness, or coldness are no more really in them than sickness or pain is in man. Take away the sensation of them; let not the eyes see light or colours, nor the ears hear sounds; let the palate not taste, nor the nose smell; and all colours, tastes, odours and sounds vanish and are reduced to their causes–i.e. bulk, figure and motion of parts.

III-Various Faculties of the Mind

What perception is everyone will know better by reflecting on what he does himself when he sees, hears, feels, tastes, smells or thinks, than by any discourse of mine.

We ought further to consider concerning perceptions, that the ideas we receive by sensation are often in grown people altered by the judgement without our taking any notice of it.

When we set before our eyes a round globe of uniform colour–e.g. gold, alabaster or jet–the idea thereby imprinted in our mind is of a flat circle variously shadowed with several degrees of light and brightness coming to our eyes.

But we, having by use been accustomed to perceive what kind of appearances convex bodies are wont to make in us, what alterations are made in the reflections of light by the difference of the sensible figures of bodies, the judgement presently, by an habitual custom, alters the appearances into their causes; so that from that which is truly a variety of shadow or colour collecting the figure, it makes it pass for a mark of figure, and frames to itself the perception of a convex figure and a uniform colour, when the idea we receive from thence is only a plane variously coloured, as is evident in painting.

Perception, then, is the first operation of our intellectual faculties, and the inlet of all knowledge into our minds.

The next faculty of the mind whereby it makes a further progress towards knowledge is that which I call retention, or the keeping of those simple ideas which from sensation or reflection it hath received. This is done, first, by keeping the idea which is brought into it for some time actually in view, which is called contemplation. The other way of retention is the power to revive again in our minds those ideas which after imprinting have disappeared, or have been, as it were, laid aside out of sight; and thus we do when we conceive heat or light, yellow or sweet, the object being removed. This is memory, the store-house of our ideas.

Another faculty we may take notice of in our minds is that of discerning and distinguishing between the several ideas it has. It is not enough to have a confused perception of something in general. Unless the mind had a distinct perception of different objects and their qualities, it would be capable of very little knowledge, even though the bodies that affect us were as busy about us as they are now, and though the mind were continually employed in thinking.

On this faculty of distinguishing one thing from another depend the evidence and certainty of several even very general propositions which have passed for innate truths, because men, overlooking the true cause why those proportions find universal assent, impute it wholly to native uniform impressions; whereas it, in truth, depends upon this clear discerning faculty of the mind, whereby it perceives two ideas to be the same or to be different.

The comparing of ideas one with another is the operation of the mind upon which depends all that large tribe of ideas comprehended under relations. The next operation is composition, whereby the mind puts together several simple ideas and combines them into complex ones.

The use of words being to stand as outward marks of our internal ideas, and those ideas being taken from particular things, if every particular idea that we take in should have a distinct name, names must be endless. To prevent this, the mind makes the particular ideas received from particular objects to become general, which is done by considering them as they are in the mind, and such appearances separate from all other existences and from the circumstances of real existence, as time, place, or any other concomitant ideas.

This is called abstraction, whereby ideas taken from particular being become general representatives of all of the same kind.

Thus, the same colour being observed to-day in chalk or snow which the mind yesterday received from milk, it considers that that appearance alone makes it a representative of all of that kind; and having given it the name 'whiteness,' it by that sound signifies the same quality wheresoever imagined or met with; and thus universals, whether ideas or terms, are made.

As the mind is wholly passive in the reception of all its simple ideas, so it exerts several acts of its own, whereby, out of its simple ideas, as the materials and foundations of the rest the others are framed. And I believe we shall find, if we observe the originals of our notions, that even the most abstruse ideas, how remote soever they may seen from sense, or from any operation of our minds, are yet only such as the understanding frames to itself, by repeating and joining together ideas that it had either from objects of sense or from its own operations about them; so that even those large and abstract ideas are derived from sensation or reflection, being no other than what the mind, by the ordinary use of its own faculties employed about ideas received from objects of sense, or from the operations it observes in itself about them, may and does attain. This may be shown in our ideas of space, time and infinity, and some others that seem the most remote from these originals.

IV-Our Knowledge of the Existence of Other Things

It is the actual receiving of ideas from without that gives us notice of the existence of other things, and makes us know that something does exist at that time without us which causes that idea in us, though perhaps we neither know nor consider how it does it. And this, though not so certain as our own intuitive knowledge, or as the deductions of our reason employed about the clear abstract ideas of our own minds, yet deserves the name of knowledge.

It is plain that those perceptions are produced by exterior causes affecting our senses for the following reasons:

Because those that lack the physical organs of any sense never can have the ideas belonging to that sense produced in their minds.

Because sometimes I find I cannot avoid having those ideas produced in my mind; for as when my eyes are shut, or the windows fast, I can at pleasure recall to my mind the ideas of light or the sun which former sensations have lodged in my memory; so I can at pleasure lay by that idea and take into my view that of a rose or taste of sugar. But if I turn my eyes at noon towards the sun, I cannot avoid the ideas which the light or sun produces in me. There is nobody who does not perceive the difference in himself contemplating the sun as he has an idea of it in his memory and actually looking upon it, of which two his perception is so distinct that few of his ideas are more distinguishable one from another; and, therefore, he has certain knowledge that they are not both memory or the action of his mind and fancies only within him, but that actual seeing has a cause without.

Add to this that many of those ideas are produced with pain, which afterwards we remember without the least offence.

Lastly, our senses bear witness to the truth of each other's report concerning the existence of sensible things without us and around us.

CARDINAL RICHELIEU OF FRANCE
(1585-1642)

"The Prince must be powerful by his reputation."

Richelieu was born in Paris in 1585. His writings indicate he desired a military career, but to foster the holdings of his influential family he studied theology and was ordained a bishop at the age of twenty-two. He was elected to the French Legislature in 1614 (The Estates General), and became a favorite of Marie de Medici, the Queen Mother of France. Marie had little practical political experience and relied on Richelieu to shape foreign policy. In 1616 he was named Secretary of State and embarked on a campaign to enhance the power of the French state. All was not smooth sailing for Richelieu; at one point Marie attempted his removal, but Richelieu's friends at court proved to be too powerful.

Richelieu promoted the power of the Royal Court of young Louis XIII by arranging a marriage between the king's sister Henrietta Maria and Charles I of England. This marriage was to have important implications for both the French and English crowns. He also sought to check the power of the Spanish and Austrian Hapsburgs, even going so far as to side with Protestant factions in the Thirty Years War. In the domestic realm, he truncated the Edict of Nantes by taking away the Huguenots' right to hold certain key fortified cities.

Richelieu's Political Will and Testament expresses a decidedly Machiavellian approach to politics. In his view power and fear are two key ingredients for effective rule by the prince. Richelieu's policies of state paved the way for the great Sun King, Louis XIV.

(Cardinal Richelieu (1585-1642) served as chief minister to the king of France for eighteen years. His policies did much to promote the concept of absolutism in France.)

Richelieu's Political Will and Testament

Power being one of the most necessary ingredients towards the grandeur of kings, and the prosperity of their governments; those who have the chief management of affairs are particularly obliged not to omit anything which may contribute to authorize their master so far as to make all the world reject him. As goodness is the object of love, power is the cause of dread: and it is most certain, that among all the princes who are capable to stir a state, fear grounded upon esteem and reverence has so much force, that it engages everyone to perform his duty.

If this principle is of great efficacy in respect to the internal part of states, it is to the full as prevailing abroad: subjects and strangers looking with the same eyes upon a formidable power, both the one and the other abstain from offending a prince, whom they are sensible is in a condition to hurt them, if he were so inclined.

I have observed by the by, that the ground of the power I am speaking of must be esteem and respect;...that when it is grounded upon any other principle, it is very dangerous; in the case instead of creating a reasonable fear, it inclines men to hate princes, who are never in a worse condition than when it turns to public aversion.

The power which induces men to respect and fear princes with love...is a tree which has divers branches, which all draw their nutriment and substance from one and the same root.

The Prince must be powerful by his reputation.

By a reasonable army always kept on foot.

And by a notable sum of money in his coffers, to supply unexpected exigencies, which often come to pass when they are least expected.

Finally, by the possession of his subjects' hearts....
(Source: Armand Jean du Pleses, Duc de Richelieu, Vol. II, Political Will and Testament London, 1695)

JACQUES BENIGNE BOSSUET

(1627-1704)

"I counsel thee to keep the king's commandment, and that in regard of the oath of God."

Bossuet was born in Dijon, France, in 1627. He was trained in the humanities and eventually obtained a doctorate in theology from the University of Paris in 1648. Ordained as a priest in 1652, he quickly obtained a reputation as a great preacher of the word of God. In 1670 he was appointed as a tutor to the Dauphin (the future Louis XIV) and evidently approached his work with great ardor. Upon completion of his duties as a precept, Bossuet was appointed Bishop in 1681.

Bossuet's Sermons are still read, but his place in history lies primarily with his work On the Divine Right of Kings. Bossuet, a proponent of the concept of the divine right of kings, identified the rule of Louis XIV as identical to the will of God, the king being seen as God's agent on earth. Bossuet quoted both Old and New Testament scripture to support his position. In Bossuet's words, "you see the image of God in the King, and you have the idea of royal majesty." Bossuet, then, provides the perfect rationale for the rule of Louis XIV, a royal monarch whose ego knew no bounds.

(Jacques-Bénigne Bossuet (1627-1704) was a court preacher for Louis XIV. Loyal to his king, Bossuet defended the divine right of kings.)

Bossuet on the Divine Right of Kings

The royal power is absolute.... The prince need render account of his acts to no one. "I counsel thee to keep the king's commandment, and that in regard of the oath of God. Be not hasty to go out of his sight; stand not on an evil thing for he doeth whatsoever pleaseth him. Where the word of a king is, there is power; and who may say unto him, What doest thou? Whoso keepeth the commandment shall feel no evil thing" [Eccles. 8:2-5]. Without this absolute authority the king could neither do good nor repress evil. It is necessary that his power be such that no one can hope to escape him, and finally, the only protection of individuals against the public authority should be their innocence. This confirms the teaching of St. Paul: "Wilt thou then not be afraid of the power? Do that which is good" [Rom. 13.3].

God is infinite, God is all. The prince, as prince, is not regarded as a private person: he is a public personage, all the state is in him; the will of all the people is included in his. As all perfection and all strength are united in God, so all the power of individuals is united in God, so all the power of individuals is united in the person of the prince. What grandeur that a single man should embody so much!...

Behold an immense people united in a single person; behold this holy power, paternal and absolute; behold the secret cause which governs the whole body of the state, contained in a single head: you see the image of God in the king, and you have the idea of royal majesty. God is holiness itself, goodness itself, and power itself. In these things lies the majesty of God. In the image of these things lies the majesty of the prince.
(From the writings of Bossuet)
(Under Louis XIV absolutism reached its peak. In 1746, the duc de Saint Simon wrote a description of Louis XIV.)

Saint Simon on Louis XIV

Louis XIV's vanity was without limit or restraint; it colored everything and convinced him that no one even approached him in military talents, in plans and enterprises, and in government. Hence, those pictures and inscriptions in the gallery at Versailles which disgust every foreigner; those opera prologues that he himself tried to sing; that flood of prose and verse in his praise for which his appetite was insatiable; those dedications of statues copied from pagan sculpture, and the insipid and sickening compliments that were continually offered to him in person and which he swallowed with unfailing relish; hence, his distaste for all merit, intelligence, education, and, most of all, independence of character and sentiment in others; his mistakes of judgment in matters of importance; his familiarity and favor reserved entirely for those to whom he felt himself superior in acquirements and ability; and, above everything else, a jealousy of his own authority which determined and took precedence over every other sort of justice, reason, and consideration whatever.

(From the writings of Saint Simon)

LOUIS XIV, KING OF FRANCE

(1638-1715)

"I am the state...."

Louis XIV was born at Saint-German-en Laye in 1638. He ascended to the throne at the age of five in 1643. His mother served as regent, ruling France until Louis came of age. Most of the decisions of state were made by Jules Cardinal Mazarin who served as the principal minister for the Queen Mother, and later for Louis. Mazarin's principal accomplishment was to bring France through the Thirty Years War (1618-1648). Mazarin spent a good deal of time tutoring Louis in the intricacies of foreign affairs. He also convinced Louis of the need to maintain a strong monarchy, a lesson young Louis XIV took to heart.

During the early years of his reign the country was rocked by a series of rebellions known as the Fronde. At one point young Louis witnessed a riot just under his palace window. These rebellions, which emanated from the nobility and spread to the masses, convinced Louis to move the center of royal government outside Paris. Louis decided to build a royal palace at Versailles, some twelve miles outside the city. Louis brought the nobility to Versailles in order to keep them under his watch. Noblemen fought desperately to adhere to every whim of the king. However, in building Versailles and by spending lavishly on the royal court, Louis created huge deficits.

Four major wars were fought during the reign of Louis XIV. Along with his war minister the Marquis de Louvois, Louis spent enormous sums on his military. The size of the French army grew to over four hundred thousand under Louis XIV, but his wars proved to be only marginally successful for France.

The enormous funds spent on the royal court and the numerous wars fought by the French army stretched the resources of France. Louis considered these costs as the price of being a great monarch. He sought to increase the power of his monarchy and saw no reason to limit his desires in relation to domestic or foreign policy. When Louis stated, "I am the state," he was echoing the Machiavellian principle that the king and state are synonymous. The desires of the Prince, indeed the needs of the Prince, were necessary to make France the greatest power in all of Europe. While the rest of Europe stood in awe of this great king in all his grandeur, the seeds for future revolution were being sown.

Louis XIV on His Role as King

Kings are absolute lords and have a full and inherent right to dispose of all property, secular and ecclesiastical alike, and to employ them as wise stewards, namely, according to the needs of their state....

Although a prince's honor compels him to keep his word, prudence does not allow him to place absolute reliance on that of others; and because he is incapable of deceiving anyone, he must not believe himself incapable of being deceived....
(From the writings of Louis XIV)

PART THREE

NICOLAUS COPERNICUS
(1473-1543)

"At Last I began to chafe that philosophers could by no means agree on any one certain theory of mechanism of the Universe..."

Copernicus was born in 1473 in Thorn, Poland. He came from a family of upper middle class means. Many of his family were merchants or government officials. Copernicus studied the liberal arts at Krakow University and later studied church canon law in Italy at the University of Bologna. While studying at the University of Bologna, Copernicus came in contact with a mathematics professor by the name of Domenico Maria de Novara. Copernicus and Novara collaborated on several projects including the observance of an eclipse of the moon by the star Aldebaran in 1497.

Copernicus returned to Poland in 1503 and wrote several treatises on ethics and morals over the next decade of his life. In 1517 Copernicus began work on his most important book, *On the Revolutions of the Heavenly Spheres*. The work was completed in 1530 but was not published until the last year of Copernicus's life in 1543. Copernicus had good reasons for not publishing his work immediately. He put forth a heliocentric theory of the Universe that contradicted the prevailing geocentric theory of this time. Church canon was centered on the geocentric model, and as Galileo was to find out almost a century later, Church canon changes only with the greatest difficulty. Most of what Copernicus communicated was intended for scientific debate and not the general population. By 1600 Copernican theory had only a few converts. By the mid-seventeenth century, after alterations to the theory by Brahe, Kepler, and Galileo the Copernican model held great sway in the scientific community. By the early eighteenth century virtually all learned men held the Copernican model, with its subsequent alternations, to be fact.

(Copernicus published On the Revolution of the Heavenly Spheres *in 1543. Copernicus was in a sense guided by the Renaissance way of thinking. That is to say he was able to "doubt" conventional thinking with a degree of confidence.)*

Copernicus On the Movement of the Earth

I may well presume, most Holy Father, that certain people, as soon as they hear that in this book about the Revolutions of the Spheres of the Universe I ascribe movement to the earthly globe, will cry out that, holding such views, I should at once be hissed off the stage....

So I should like your Holiness to know that I was induced to think of a method of computing the motions of the spheres by nothing else than the knowledge that the Mathematicians [who had previously considered the problem] are inconsistent in these investigations.

For, first, the mathematicians are so unsure of the movements of the Sun and the Moon that they cannot even explain or observe the constant length of the seasonal year. Secondly, in determining the motions of these and of the other five planets, they use neither the same principles and hypotheses nor the same demonstrations of the apparent motions and revolutions.... Nor have they been able thereby to discern or deduce the principal thing–namely the shape of the Universe and the unchangeable symmetry of its parts....

I pondered long upon this uncertainty of mathematical tradition in establishing the motions of the system of the spheres. As last I began to chafe that philosophers could by no means agree on any one certain theory of the mechanism of the Universe, wrought for us by a supremely good and orderly Creator.... I therefore took pains to read again the works of the philosophers on whom I could lay hand to seek out whether any of them had ever supposed that the motions of the spheres were other than those demanded by the [ptolemaic] mathematical schools. I found first in Cicero that Hicetas [of Syracuse, fifth century B.C.] had realized that the Earth moved. Afterwards I found in Plutarch that certain others had held the like opinion.... Thus assuming motions, which in my work I ascribe to the Earth, by long and frequent observations I have at last discovered that, if the motions of the rest of the planets be brought into relation with the circulation of the Earth and be reckoned in proportion to the circles of each planet, not only do their phenomena presently ensue, but the orders and magnitudes of all stars and spheres, nay the heavens themselves, become so bound together that nothing in any part thereof could be moved from its place without producing confusion of all the other parts of the Universe as a whole. (From: Copernicus' *On the Revolutions of Heavenly Spheres.*)

GALILEO GALILEI

(1564-1642)

"For the Bible is not chained in every expression to conditions as strict as those which govern all physical effects; nor is God any less excellently revealed in nature's actions than in the sacred statements of the Bible...."

Galileo was one of the founders of modern science. University professor (at Pisa and at Padua in Italy), astronomer, mathematician, and physicist, he posed serious challenges to the accepted views of his time, dominated as those views were by the orthodoxy of the Roman Catholic Church and the centuries-old influence of Aristotle. It is in Galileo's career that the long-simmering conflict between religion and science finally ignited.

His achievements were both theoretical and practical, as he produced thorough, reasoned arguments concerning dynamics and mechanics and invented major instruments (a useful telescope, the thermometer, and an improved microscope) to further the development of what was emerging as modern scientific inquiry.

The most dramatic moment in the struggle between faith and reason, as that struggle was personified by Galileo, came in 1632, when Galileo, then sixty-eight, published *Dialogues Concerning the Two Chief World Systems*. His defense of the Copernican system, which held that the earth orbited the sun, opposing the view held by the church, resulted in his imprisonment, trial, and conviction for heresy. Publicly, he recanted his views; privately, he never relinquished them. He was not severely punished, spending the last decade of his life developing his scientific theories.

(Galileo, who supported the Copernican view of science, nevertheless felt that science and the Church were compatible. Galileo argued that God was revealed through nature. In 1633 the Roman Catholic church condemned Galileo.)

Galileo on Science and the Bible (1615)

The reason produced for condemning the opinion that the earth moves and the sun stands still is that in many places in the Bible one may read that the sun moves and the earth stands still....

With regard to this argument, I think in the first place that it is very pious to say and prudent to affirm that the holy Bible can never speak untruth–whenever its true meaning is understood. But I believe nobody will deny that it is often very abstruse, and may say things which are quite different from what its bare words signify....

Thus being granted, I think that in discussions of physical problems we ought to begin not from the authority of scriptural passages, but from sense experiences and necessary demonstrations; for the holy Bible and the phenomena of nature proceed alike from the divine Word, the former as the dictate of the Holy Ghost and the latter as the observant executrix of God's commands. It is necessary for the Bible, in order to be accommodated to the understanding of every man, to speak many things which appear to differ from the absolute truth so far as the bare meaning of the words is concerned. But Nature, on the other hand, is inexorable and immutable; she never transgresses the laws imposed upon her, or cares a whit whether her abstruse reasons and methods of operation are understandable to men. For that reason it appears that nothing physical which sense-experience sets before our eyes, or which necessary demonstrations prove to us, ought to be called in question (much less condemned) upon the testimony of biblical passages which may have some different meaning beneath their words. For the Bible is not chained in every expression to conditions as strict as those which govern all physical effects; nor is God any less excellently revealed in Nature's actions than in the sacred statements of the Bible....

From this I do not mean to infer that we need not have an extraordinary esteem for the passages of holy Scripture. On the contrary, having arrived at any certainties in physics, we ought to utilize these as the most appropriate aids in the true exposition of the Bible and in the investigation of those meanings which are necessarily contained therein for these must be concordant with demonstrated truths. I should judge the authority of the Bible was designed to persuade men of those articles and propositions which, surpassing all human reasoning, could not be made credible by science, or by any other means than through the very mouth of the Holy Spirit....

But I do not feel obliged to believe that the same God who has endowed us with senses, reason, and intellect had intended to forgo their use and by some other means to give us knowledge which we can attain by them.

(From Galileo's writings in 1615)

FRANCIS BACON

(1561-1626)

"There are four classes of idols which beset men's minds. To these, for distinction's sake, I have assigned names,—calling the first class Idols of the Tribe; the second, Idols of the Cave; the third, Idols of the Market-place; the fourth, Idols of the Theater.

Along with René Descartes Sir Francis Bacon was one of the wellsprings of modern thought. A man of diverse interests–science, politics, literature–Bacon sought to bring to an end the stifling authority of the past, arguing that "knowledge is power" and that the benefits to be derived from such power were being denied to human beings by their submission to the false and outdated concepts of an unscientific intellectual tradition.

In his *Novum Organum* (New Method) he attacked what he believed to be the false idols that dominate and restrict human understanding.

NOVUM ORGANUM FRANCIS BACON

xxxvii

The doctrine of those who have denied that certainty could be attained at all, has some agreement with my way of proceeding at the first setting out; but they end in being infinitely separated and opposed. For the holders of that doctrine assert simply that nothing can be known; I also assert that not much can be known in nature by the way which is now in use. But then they go on to destroy the authority of the senses and understanding; whereas I proceed to devise and supply helps for the same.

xxxviii

The idols and false notions which are now in possession of the human understanding, and have taken deep root therein, not only so beset men's minds that truth can hardly find entrance, but even after entrance obtained, they will again in the very instauration of the sciences meet and trouble us, unless men being forewarned of the danger fortify themselves as far as may be against their assaults.

xxxix

There are four classes of idols which beset men's minds. To these for distinction's sake I have assigned names,—calling the first class *Idols of the Tribe*; the second, *Idols of the Cave*; the third, *Idols of the Marketplace*; the fourth, *Idols of the Theater*.

xl

The formation of ideas and axioms by true induction is no doubt the proper remedy to be applied for the keeping off and clearing away of idols. To point them out, however, is of great use, for the doctrine of idols is to the interpretation of nature what the doctrine of the refutation of sophisms is to common logic.

xli

The Idols of the Tribe have their foundation in human nature itself, and in the tribe or race of men. For it is a false assertion that the sense of man is the measure of things. On the contrary, all perceptions, as well of the sense as of the mind, are according to the measure of the individual and not according to the measure of the universe. And the human understanding is like a false mirror, which, receiving rays irregularly, distorts and discolors the nature of things by mingling its own nature with it.

xlii

The Idols of the Cave are the idols of the individual man. For everyone (besides the errors common to human nature in general) has a cave or den of his own, which refracts and discolors the light of nature; owing either to his own proper and peculiar nature or to his education and conversation with others; or to the reading of books, and the authority of those whom he esteems and admires; or to the differences of impressions, accordingly as they take place in a mind preoccupied and predisposed or in a mind indifferent and settled; or the like. So that the spirit of man (according as it is meted out to different individuals) is in fact a thing variable and full of perturbation, and governed as it were by chance. Whence it was well observed by Heraclitus that men look for sciences in their own lesser worlds, and not in the greater or common world.

xliii

There are also idols formed by the intercourse and association of men with each other, which I call Idols of the Market-place, on account of the commerce and consort of men there. For it is by discourse that men associate; and words are imposed according to the apprehension of the vulgar. And therefore the ill and unfit choice of words wonderfully obstructs the understanding. Nor do the definitions or explanations wherewith in some things learned men are wont to guard and defend themselves, by any means set the matter right. But words plainly force and overrule the understanding, and throw all into confusion, and lead men away into numberless empty controversies and idle fancies.

xliv

Lastly, there are idols which have immigrated into men's minds from the various dogmas of philosophies, and also from wrong laws of demonstration. These I call Idols of the Theater: because in my judgment all the received systems are but so many stage-plays, representing worlds of their own creation after an unreal and scenic fashion. Nor is it only of the systems now in vogue, or only of the ancient sects and philosophies, that I speak: for many more plays of the same kind may yet be composed and in like artificial manner set forth: seeing that errors the most widely different have nevertheless causes for the most part alike. Neither again do I mean this only of entire systems, but also of many principles and axioms in science. Which by tradition, credulity, and negligence have come to be received.

But of these several kinds of idols I must speak more largely and exactly, that the understanding may be duly cautioned.

ISAAC NEWTON

(1642-1727)

"Nature is pleased with simplicity, and affects not the pomp of superfluous causes."

Isaac Newton was born in Woolsthrorpe, Lincolnshire, England in 1642. Because Newton's family was of the middle class, he was afforded an excellent education. Newton was a precocious child who constantly built things such as windmills, clocks, special flying kites, etc. Newton, however, dismissed his early schooling as unable to hold his direct attention. Fortunately, Newton showed enough intellectual promise that he was admitted to the University of Cambridge, Trinity College, in 1661. At Trinity College he showed an exceptional aptitude for mathematics and astronomy. Newton's professors generally recognized his genius and took special care to promote his interests in mathematics. Newton was graduated from Cambridge in 1665.

It did not take Newton long to make his impact on the world. After leaving Cambridge, Newton began his work on what he called the "method of fluxions." This work would lead to the development of Calculus. In addition, Newton began his work on the effects of gravity. In time his gravitational theories would provide a precise calculation of the movement of the planets. Newton also contributed directly to our understanding of the nature of light. Through his various elements with prisms, he was about to demonstrate that light was composed of many colors caused by refraction. By the time Newton returned to Cambridge as a professor in 1667, he had already earned a reputation as a scientist of the first order.

Newton's first published work appeared in 1672 when he announced his theory of optics. In 1687 Newton published his *Principia Mathematica* in which he outlined his theory relating to planetary orbits. The book became an instant sensation in the scientific community. In addition to explaining the movements of the solar system, the work proved to be an invaluable tool in explaining natural phenomena such as tidal movements and the variations in seasonal changes from year to year.

In 1703 Newton left Cambridge and took up the position as president of the Royal Society, a position he would hold until the last days of his life. In 1705 he was knighted by Queen Anne. Voltaire would later write of witnessing the funeral of Sir Isaac Newton, which he at first mistook as the funeral of a prince because of the great pomp and circumstance of the funeral procession. Voltaire writes that he was overwhelmed with emotion when he learned it was the funeral of the great Newton, a man of science.

(Isaac Newton must be considered one of the most important men in world history. Newton's Rules of Reasoning *helped to develop the scientific method of research.)*

Newton's Rules of Reasoning (1687)

Rule I. We are to admit no more causes of natural things than such as are both true and sufficient to explain their appearances.

To this purpose the philosophers say that Nature does nothing in vain, and more is in vain when less will serve; for Nature is pleased with simplicity, and affects not the pomp of superfluous causes.

Rule II. Therefore to the same natural effects we must, as far as possible, assign the same causes.

As to respiration in a man and in a beast; the descent of stones in Europe and in America; the light of our culinary fire and of the sun; the reflection of light in the earth, and in the planets.

Rule III. The qualities of bodies, which admit neither intension nor remission of degrees, and which are found to belong to all bodies within the reach of our experiments, are to be esteemed the universal qualities of all bodies whatsoever.

For since the qualities of bodies are only known to us by experiments, we are to hold for universal all such as universally agree with experiments and such as are not liable to diminution can never be quite taken away. We are certainly not to relinquish the evidence of experiments for the sake of dreams and vain fictions of our own devising.... We no other way know the extension of bodies than by our senses, nor do these reach it in all bodies; but because we perceive extension in all that are sensible, therefore we ascribe it universally to all others also.

That abundance of bodies are hard, we learn by experience; and because the hardness of the whole arises from the hardness of the parts, we therefore justly infer the hardness of the undivided particles not only of the bodies we feel but of all others. That bodies are impenetrable, we gather not from reason, but from sensation....

Lastly, if it universally appears, by experiments and astronomical observations, that all bodies about the earth gravitate towards the earth, and that in proportion to the quantity of matter which they severally contain; ...we must, in consequence of this rule, universally allow that all bodies whatsoever are endowed with a principle of universal gravitation....

Rule IV. In experimental philosophy we are to look upon propositions collected by general induction from phaenomena as accurately or very nearly true, notwithstanding any contrary hypotheses that may be imagined, till such time as other phaenomena occur, by which they may either be made more accurate, or liable to exceptions.

This rule must follow, that the argument of induction may not be evaded by hypotheses.

BLAISE PASCAL

(1623-62)

"A thinking reed–it is not from space that I must seek my dignity, but from the government of my thought."

    Blaise Pascal was born in Clermont-Ferrand, France in 1623. He exhibited an aptitude for mathematics at a very young age. By the age of sixteen he had formulated important ideas in the area of geometry. This work later became known as Pascal's theorem. At the age of nineteen he developed the world's first mechanical adding machine. Additionally, Pascal did important work relating to atmospheric pressure and to mathematical probability. Pascal is also noted for having promoted the empirical method of scientific discovery. The empirical method put forth by Pascal emphasized the need for observation via experimentation. While he did not abandon prevailing analytical methods altogether, he promoted the experimental method as the true way of scientific discovery.

    Pascal is also noted for his religious writings. Perhaps his most read work today is his *Pensees*, which outline his thoughts on religion. Pascal was a proponent of that branch of Catholicism known as Jansenism, which stressed that revelation is obtainable only by faith. There is, in fact, a connection between Pascal's work in mathematical probability and his faith. In his famous wager, which concerns whether we should believe in God, he states, "As for me I bet on God, if he exists you win all, if He does not, you lose nothing."

    At the heart of Pascal's method is the application of skepticism to matters of science. For anything to be accepted as true science it must meet the rigorous demands of the scientific method. However, in matters of religion, Pascal relies on faith to carry him through.

(Blaise Pascal is another example of a seventeenth century writer/scientist with a religious bent. Pascal, however, was somewhat pessimistic about the new scientific discoveries.)

Pascal on Thinking Creatures

I can well conceive a man without hands, feet, head (for it is only experience which teaches us that the head is more necessary than feet). But I cannot conceive man without thought; he would be a stone or a brute.

Reason commands us far more imperiously than a master; for in disobeying the one we are unfortunate, and in disobeying the other we are fools.

Man is but a reed, the most feeble thing in nature; but he is a thinking reed. The entire universe need not arm itself to crush him. A vapour, a drop of water suffices to kill him, but, if the universe were to crush him, man would still be more noble than that which killed him, because he knows that he dies and the advantage which the universe has over him; the universe knows nothing of this.

All our dignity consists, then, in thought. By it we must elevate ourselves, and not by space and time which we cannot fill. Let us endeavor, then, to think well: this is the principle of morality.

A thinking reed-it is not from space that I must seek my dignity, but from the government of my thought. I shall have no more if I possess worlds. By space the universe encompasses and swallows me up like an atom; by thought I comprehend the world.
(From Pascal's writings)

RENE DESCARTES

(1596-1650)

"I had long since remarked that in matters of conduct it is necessary sometimes to follow opinions known to be uncertain, as if they were not subject to doubt; but, because now I was desirous to devote myself to the search after truth, I considered that I must do just the contrary, and reject as absolutely false everything concerning which I could imagine the least doubt to exist."

Many historians of philosophy agree that modern philosophy began with Descartes. In his emphasis on the usefulness of mathematics, in his reliance on individual intellectual autonomy, he established the rational skepticism that became the prevailing temperament of thinkers after his time.

As a young student he excelled because he had faith in the knowledge transmitted to him in the classroom. But his true brilliance emerged as his growing doubt about the worth of the knowledge he had mastered led him to the liberating experience of embracing the power of his own mind.

In *Discourse on Method* Descartes offers a highly readable account of the evolution of his own thought processes and, by extension, provides a preview of the intellectual development which was to follow in Europe and America.

DISCOURSE ON METHOD
RENÉ DESCARTES

I-The Aim of the Discourse

Good sense or reason must be better distributed than anything else in the world, for no man desires more of it than he already has. This shows that reason is by nature equal in all men. If there is diversity of opinion, this arises from the fact that we conduct our thought by different ways and consider not the same things. It does not suffice that the understanding be good–it must be well applied.

My mind is no better than another's, but I have been lucky enough to chance on certain ways, which have led me to a certain method by means of which it seems to me that I may by degrees augment my knowledge to the modest measure of my intellect and my length of days. I shall be very glad to make plain in this Discourse the paths I have followed, and to picture my life so that all may judge of it, and by the setting forth of their opinions may furnish me with yet other means of improvement.

It is my design not to teach the method which each man ought to follow for the right guidance of his reason, but only to show in what manner I have tried to conduct my own.

I have been nourished on letters from my infancy, but as soon as I had finished the customary course of study, I found myself hampered by so many doubts and errors that I seemed to have reaped no benefits, except that I had observed more and more of my ignorance. Yet I was at one of the most celebrated schools in Europe, and I was not held inferior to my fellow-students, some of whom were destined to take the place of our masters; nor did our age seem less fruitful of good wits than any which had gone before.

Though I did not cease to esteem the studies of the schools, I began to think that I had given enough time to languages, enough also to ancient books, their stories and their fables; for when a man spends too much time in travelling abroad, he becomes a stranger in his own country; and so, when he is too curious concerning what went on in past ages, he is apt to remain ignorant of what is taking place in his own day. I set a high price on eloquence, and I was in love with poetry; I rejoiced in mathematics, but knew nothing of its true use.

I revered our theology, but, since the way to heaven lies open to the ignorant no less than to the learned, and the revealed truths which lead thither are beyond our intelligence, I did not dare to submit them to my feeble reasonings.

In philosophy there is no truth which is not disputed and which, consequently, is not doubtful; the other sciences all borrow their principles from philosophy.

Therefore, I entirely gave up the study of letters and employed the rest of my youth in travelling, being resolved to seek no other science than that which I might find within myself, or in the great Book of the World.

Here the best lesson that I learnt was not to believe too firmly anything of which I had learnt merely by example and custom; and thus little by little was delivered from many errors which are liable to obscure the light of nature and to diminish our capacity of hearing reason. Finally, I resolved one day to study myself in the same way, and in this it seems to me I succeeded much better than if I had never departed from either my country or my books.

II-The Intellectual Crisis

Being in Germany, on my way to rejoin the army after the coronation of the Emperor [Ferdinand II], I was lying at an inn where, in default of other conversation, I was at liberty to entertain my own thoughts. Of these, one of the first was that often there is less perfection in works which are composite than in those which issue from a single hand. Such was the case with buildings, cities, states; for a people which has made its laws from time to time to meet particular occasions will enjoy a less perfect polity than a people which from the beginning has observed the constitution of a farsighted legislator. This is very certain, that the estate of true religion, which God alone has ordained, must be incomparably better guided than any other.

And again, I considered that as, during our childhood, we had been governed by our appetites and our tutors, which are often at variance, which neither of them perhaps always gave us the best counsel, it is almost impossible that our judgments should be so pure and so solid as they would have been if we had had the perfect use of our reason from the time of our birth and had never been guided by anything else.

Hence, as regarded the opinions that I had received into my belief, I thought that, as a private person may pull down his own house to build a finer, so I could not do better than remove them therefrom in order to replace them by sounder, or, after I should have adjusted them to the level of reason, to establish the same once more.

When I was younger I had studied logic, analytical geometry and algebra. Of these, I found that logic served rather for explaining things we already know; while of geometry and algebra, the former is so tied to the consideration of figures that it cannot exercise the understanding without wearying the imagination, and the latter is so bound down to certain rules and ciphers that it has been made a confused and obscure art which hampers the mind instead of a science which cultivates it. And as a state is better governed which has but few laws, and those strictly observed, I believed that I should find sufficient these four precepts:

The first was never to accept anything as true when I did not recognize it clearly to be so–that is to say, carefully to avoid precipitation and prejudice, but to include in my opinions nothing beyond that which should present itself so clearly and distinctly to my mind that I might have no occasion to doubt it.

The second was to divide up the difficulties which I should examine into as many parts as possible, and as should be required for their better resolution.

The third was to conduct my thoughts in order, by beginning with the simplest objects, so as to mount little by little, by stages, to the most complex knowledge, even supposing an order among things which did not naturally stand in an order of antecedent and consequent.

And the last was to make everywhere enumerations so complete, and surveys so wide, that I should be sure of omitting nothing.

Exact observation of these precepts gave me such facility in unravelling the questions comprehended in geometrical analysis and in algebra, that in two or three months not only did I find my way through many which I had formerly accounted too hard for me, but towards the end, I seemed to be able to determine, in those which were new to me, by what means and to what extent it was possible to resolve them.

And so I promised myself that I would apply my system with equal success to the difficulties of other sciences; but since their principles must all be borrowed from philosophy, in which I found no certain principles of its own, I thought that before all else I must try to establish some therein. By way of preparation (for I was then but twenty-three years old) I must root up from my mind my previous bad opinion of it, and must practise my method in order that I might be confirmed in it.

III-A Rule of Life

Meanwhile I must have a rule of life as a shelter while my new house was in building, and this consisted of three or four maxims.

The first was to conform myself to the laws and customs of my country and to hold to the religion in which, by God's grace, I had been brought up; guiding myself, for the rest, by the least extreme opinions of the most intelligent. Among extremes I counted all promises by which a man curtails anything of his liberty; for I should have deemed it a grave fault against good sense if, because I approved something in a given moment, I had bound myself to accept it as good for ever after.

My second maxim was to follow resolutely even doubtful opinions when sure opinions were not available, just as the traveller, lost in some forest, had better walk straight forward, though in a chance direction; for thus he will arrive, if not precisely where he desires to be, at least at a better place than the middle of a forest.

My third maxim was to endeavour always to conquer myself rather than fortune, and to change my desires rather than the order of the world, and in general to bring myself to believe that there is nothing wholly in our power except our thoughts. And I believe that herein lay the secret of those philosophers who, in the days of old, could withdraw from the domination of fortune and, despite pain and poverty, challenge the felicity of their gods.

Finally, after looking out upon the divers occupations of men, I pondered that I could do no better than persevere in that which I had chosen–so deep was my content in discovering every day by its means truths which seemed to me important, yet were unknown to the world.

Having thus made myself sure of these maxims, and having set them apart together with the verities of faith, I judged that for the rest of my opinions I might set freely to work to divest myself of them. For nine years, therefore, I went up and down the world a spectator rather than an actor. These nine years slipped away before I had begun to seek for the foundations of any philosophy more certain, nor perhaps should I have dared to undertake the quest had it not been put about that I had already succeeded.

IV- "I Think, Therefore I Am"

I had long since remarked that in matters of conduct it is necessary sometimes to follow opinions known to be uncertain, as if they were not subject to doubt; but, because now I was desirous to devote myself to the search after truth, I considered that I must do just the contrary, and reject as absolutely false everything concerning which I could imagine the least doubt to exist.

Thus, because our senses sometimes deceive us, I would suppose that nothing is such as they make us to imagine it; and because I was as likely to err as another in reasoning, I rejected as false all the reasons which I had formerly accepted as demonstrative;and finally, considering that all the thoughts we have when awake can come to us also when we sleep without any of them being true, I resolved to feign that everything which had ever entered my mind was no more truth than the illusion of my dreams.

But I observed that, while I was thus resolved to feign that everything was false, I who thought must of necessity be somewhat; and remarking this truth–*I think, therefore I am*–was so firm and so assured that all the most extravagant suppositions of the sceptics were unable to shake it, I judged that I could unhesitatingly accept it as the first principle of the philosophy I was seeking. I could feign that there was no world, I could not feign that I did not exist. And I judged that I might take it as a general rule that the things which we conceive very clearly and very distinctly are all true, and that the only difficulty lies in the way of discerning which those things are that we conceive distinctly.

After this, reflecting upon the fact that I doubted, and that consequently my being was not quite perfected (for I saw that to *know* is a greater perfection than to *doubt*), I bethought me to inquire whence I had learnt to think of something more perfect than myself; and it was clear to me that this must come from some nature which was in fact more perfect. For other things I could regard as dependencies of my nature if they were real, and if they were not real they might proceed from nothing–that is to say, they might exist in me by way of defect.

But it could not be the same with the idea of a being more perfect than my own; for to derive it from nothing was manifestly impossible; and because it is no less repugnant that the more perfect should follow and depend upon the less perfect than that something should come forth out of nothing. I could not derive it from myself.

It remained, then, to conclude that it was put into me by a nature truly more perfect than was I and possessing in itself all the perfections of what I could form an idea–in a word, by God. To which I added that, since I knew some perfections which I did not possess, I was not the only being who existed, but that there must of necessity be some other being, more perfect, on whom I depended, and from whom I had acquired all that I possessed; for if I had existed alone and independent of all other, so that I had of myself all this little whereby I participated in the Perfect Being. I should have been able to have in myself all those other qualities which I knew myself to lack, and so to be infinite, eternal, immutable, omniscient, almighty–in fine, to possess all the perfections which I could observe in God.

Proposing to myself the geometer's subject matter, and then turning again to examine my idea of a Perfect Being, I found that existence was comprehended in that idea just as in the idea of a triangle is comprehended the notion that the sum of its angles is equal to two right angles; and that consequently it is as certain that God, this Perfect Being is or exists, as any geometrical demonstration could be.

That there are many who persuade themselves that there is a difficulty in knowing Him is due to the scholastic maxim that there is nothing in the understanding which has not first been in the senses; where the ideas of God and the soul have never been.

Than the existence of God all other things, even those which it seems to a man extravagant to doubt, such as his having a body, are less certain. Nor is there any reason sufficient to remove such doubt but such as presupposes the existence of God. From His existence it follows that our ideas or notions, being real things, and coming from God, cannot but be true in so far as they are clear and distinct. In so far as they contain falsity, they are confused and obscure, there is in them an element of mere negation (*elles participent du neant*); that is to say, they are thus confused in us because we ourselves are not all perfect. And it is evident that falsity or imperfection can no more come forth from God than can perfection proceed from nothingness. But, did we not know that all which is in us of the real and the true comes from a perfect and infinite being, however clear and distinct our ideas might be, we should have no reason for assurance that they possessed the final perfection–truth.

Reason instructs us that all our ideas must have some foundation of truth, for it could not be that the All-Perfect and the All-True should otherwise have put them into us; and because our reasonings are never so evident or so complete when we sleep as when we wake, although sometimes during sleep our imagination may be more vivid and positive, it also instructs us that such truth as our thoughts have will be in our waking thoughts rather than in our dreams.

V-Why I do not Publish "the World"

I have always remained firm in my resolve to assume no other principle than that which I have used to demonstrate the existence of God and of the soul, and to receive nothing which did not seem to me clearer and more certain than the demonstrations of the philosophers had seemed before; yet not only have I found means of satisfying myself with regard to the principal difficulties which are usually treated of in philosophy, but also I have remarked certain laws which God has so established in nature, and of which He has implanted such notions in our souls, that we cannot doubt that they are observed in all which happens in the world.

The principal truths which flow from these I have tried to unfold in a treatise (On the World, or on Light), which certain considerations prevent me from publishing. This I concluded three years ago, and had begun to revise it for the printer, when I learnt that certain persons to whom I defer had disapproved an opinion on physics published a short time before by a certain person (Galileo, condemned by the Roman Inquisition in 1633), in which opinion I had noticed nothing prejudicial to religion; and this made me fear that there might be some among my opinions in which I was mistaken.

I now believe that I ought to continue to write all the things which I judge of importance, but ought in no wise to consent to their publication during my life. For my experience of the objections which might be made forbids me to hope for any profit from them. I have tried both friends and enemies, yet it has seldom happened that they have offered any objection which I had not in some measure foreseen; so that I have never, I may say, found a critic who did not seem to be either less rigorous or less fair-minded than myself.

Whereupon I gladly take this opportunity to beg those who shall come after us never to believe that the things which they are told come from me unless I have divulged them myself; and I am in nowise astonished at the extravagances attributed to those old philosophers whose writings have not come down to us. They were the greatest minds of their time, but have been ill reported.

Why, I am sure that the most devoted of those who now follow Aristotle would esteem themselves happy if they had as much knowledge of nature as he had, even on the condition that they should never have more! They are like ivy, which never mounts higher than the trees which support it, and which even comes down again after it has attained their summit. So at least, it seems to me, do they who, not content with knowing all that is explained by their author, would find in him the solution also of many difficulties of which he says nothing, and of which, perhaps, he never thought.

Yet their method of philosophising is very convenient for those who have but middling minds, for the obscurity of the distinctions and principles which they employ enables them to speak of all things as boldly as if they had knowledge of them, and sustain all they have to say against the most subtle and skillful without there being any means of convincing them; wherein they seem to me like a blind man who, in order to fight on equal terms with a man who has his sight, invites him into the depths of a cavern.

And I may say that it is to their interest that I should abstain from publishing the principles of the philosophy which I employ, for so simple and so evident are they that to publish them would be like opening windows into their caverns and letting in the day. But if they prefer acquaintance with a little truth, and desire to follow a plan like mine, there is no need for me to say to them any more in this discourse than I have already said.

For if they are capable of passing beyond what I have done, much rather will they be able to discover for themselves whatever I believe myself to have found out; besides which, the practice which they will acquire in seeking out easy things and thence passing to others which are more difficult, will stead them better than all my instructions.

But if some of the matters spoken about at the beginning of the Dioptrics and the Meteors [published with the Discourse on Method] should at first give offence because I have called them 'suppositions,' and have shown no desire to prove them, let the reader have patience to read the whole attentively, and I have hope that he will be satisfied.

The time remaining to me I have resolved to employ in trying to acquire some knowledge of nature, such that we may be able to draw from it more certain rules for medicine than those which we possess. And I hereby declare that I shall always hold myself more obliged to those by whose favour I enjoy my leisure undisturbed than I should be to any who should offer me the most esteemed employments in the world.

BENEDICT SPINOZA

(1632-1677)

"All the objects pursued by the multitude not only bring no remedy that tends to preserve our being, but even act as hindrances, causing the death not seldom of those who possess them, and always of those who are possessed by them."

Born Baruch Spinoza, this disciple of the emerging scientific rationalism, was excommunicated from his Amsterdam synagogue for heresy. Isolated from his Jewish congregation, Spinoza took the Latin form of his given name and is known to history as Benedict (Blessed). Despite what were then, and in some quarters still are, his radical views on theology, metaphysics, ethics, and politics, Spinoza acquired a small and devoted following in his lifetime. The challenging content of his ideas kept much of his work, notably his masterpiece, *The Ethics*, from being published while he was alive. *The Ethics* is a demanding, highly technical investigation into human psychology and behavior. The few pages included here are from a shorter work, "On the Improvement of the Understanding." In it Spinoza makes clear the perils of common desires and ambitions and suggests an alternative approach to life that in his view is both more rewarding and more ethical.

ON THE IMPROVEMENT OF THE UNDERSTANDING
BENEDICT SPINOZA

After experience had taught me that all the usual surroundings of social life are vain and futile; seeing that none of the objects of my fears contained in themselves anything either good or bad, except in so far as the mind is affected by them, I finally resolved to inquire whether there might be some real good having power to communicate itself, which would affect the mind singly, to the exclusion of all else: whether, in fact, there might be anything of which the discovery and attainment would enable me to enjoy continuous, supreme, and unending happiness. I say "I finally resolved," for at first sight it seemed unwise willingly to lose hold on what was sure for the sake of something then uncertain. I could see the benefits which are acquired through fame and riches, and that I should be obliged to abandon the quest for such objects, if I seriously devoted myself to the search for something different and new. I perceived that if true happiness chanced to be placed in the former I should necessarily miss it; while if, on the other hand, it were not so placed, and I gave them my whole attention, I should equally fail.

I therefore debated whether it would not be possible to arrive at the new principle, or at any rate at a certainty concerning its existence, without changing the conduct and usual plan of my life; with this end in view I made many efforts, but in vain. For the ordinary surroundings of life which are esteemed by men (as their actions testify) to be the highest good, may be classed under the three heads–Riches, Fame, and the Pleasures of Sense: with these three the mind is so absorbed that it has little power to reflect on any different good. By sensual pleasure the mind is enthralled to the extent of quiescence, as if the supreme good were actually attained, so that it is quite incapable of thinking of any other object; when such pleasure has been gratified it is followed by extreme melancholy, whereby the mind, though not enthralled, is disturbed and dulled.

The pursuit of honours and riches is likewise very absorbing, especially if such objects be sought simply for their own sake, inasmuch as they are then supposed to constitute the highest good. In the case of fame the mind is still more absorbed, for fame is conceived as always good for its own sake, and as the ultimate end to which all actions are directed. Further, the attainment of riches and fame is not followed as in the case of sensual pleasures by repentance, but, the more we acquire, the greater is our delight, and, consequently, the more are we incited to increase both the one and the other; on the other hand, if our hopes happen to be frustrated we are plunged into the deepest sadness. Fame has the further drawback that it compels its votaries to order their lives according to the opinions of their fellow-men, shunning what they usually shun, and seeking what they usually seek.

When I saw that all these ordinary objects of desire would be obstacles in the way of a search for something different and new—nay, that they were so opposed thereto, that either they or it would have to be abandoned, I was forced to inquire which would prove the most useful to me: for, as I say, I seemed to be willingly losing hold on a sure good for the sake of something uncertain. However, after I had reflected on the matter, I came in the first place to the conclusion that by abandoning the ordinary objects of pursuit, and betaking myself to a new quest, I should be leaving a good, uncertain by reason of its own nature, as may be gathered from what has been said, for the sake of a good not uncertain in its nature (for I sought for a fixed good), but only in the possibility of its attainment.

Further reflection convinced me, that if I could really get to the root of the matter I should be leaving certain evils for a certain good. I thus perceived that I was in a state of great peril, and I compelled myself to seek with all my strength for a remedy, however uncertain it might be; as a sick man struggling with a deadly disease, when he sees that death will surely be upon him unless a remedy be found, is compelled to seek such a remedy with all his strength, inasmuch as his whole hope lies therein. All the objects pursued by the multitude not only bring no remedy that tends to preserve our being, but even act as hindrances, causing the death not seldom of those who possess them, and always of those who are possessed by them. There are many examples of men who have suffered persecution even to death for the sake of their riches, and of men who in pursuit of wealth have exposed themselves to so many dangers, that they have paid away their life as a penalty for their folly. Examples are no less numerous of men, who have endured the utmost wretchedness for the sake of gaining or preserving their reputation. Lastly, there are innumerable cases of men, who have hastened their death through over-indulgence in sensual pleasure. All these evils seem to have arisen from the fact, that happiness or unhappiness is made wholly to depend on the quality of the object which we love. When a thing is not loved, no quarrels will arise concerning it–no sadness will be felt if it perishes–no envy if it is possessed by another–no fear, no hatred, in short no disturbances of the mind. All these arise from the love of what is perishable, such as the objects already mentioned. But love towards a thing eternal and infinite feeds the mind wholly with joy, and is itself unmingled with any sadness, wherefore it is greatly to be desired and sought for with all our strength. Yet it was not at random that I used the words, "If I could go to the root of the matter," for, though what I have urged was perfectly clear to my mind, I could not forthwith lay aside all love of riches, sensual enjoyment, and fame. One thing was evident, namely, that while my mind was employed with these thoughts it turned away from its former objects of desire, and seriously considered the search for a new principle; this state of things was a great comfort to me, for I perceived that the evils were not such as to resist all remedies. Although these intervals were at first rare, and of very short duration, yet afterwards, as the true good became more and more discernible to me, they became more frequent and more lasting; especially after I had recognized that the acquisition of wealth, sensual pleasure, or fame, is only a hindrance, so long as they are sought as ends not as means; if they be sought as means, they will be under restraint, and, far from being hindrances, will further not a little the end for which they are sought, as I will show in due time.

  I will here only briefly state what I mean by true good, and also what is the nature of the highest good. In order that this may be rightly understood, we must bear in mind that the terms good and evil are only applied relatively, so that the same thing may be called both good and bad, according to the relations in view, in the same way as it may be called perfect or imperfect. Nothing regarded in its own nature can be called perfect or imperfect; especially when we are aware that all things which come to pass, come to pass according to the eternal order and fixed laws of nature. However, human weakness cannot attain to this order in its own thoughts, but meanwhile man conceives a human character much more stable than his own, and sees that there is no reason why he should not himself acquire such a character. Thus he is led to seek for means which will bring him to this pitch of perfection, and calls everything which will serve as such means a true good. The chief good is that he should arrive, together with other individuals if possible, at the possession of the aforesaid character. What that character is we shall show in due time, namely, that it is the knowledge of the union existing between the mind and the whole of nature. This, then, is the end for which I strive, to attain to such a character myself, and to endeavour that many should attain to it with me. In other words, it is part of my happiness to lend a helping hand, that many others may understand even as I do, so that their understanding and desire may entirely agree with my own. In order to bring this about, it is necessary to understand as much of nature as will enable us to attain to the aforesaid character, and also to form a social order such as is most conducive to the attainment of this character by the greatest number with the least difficulty and danger. We must seek the assistance of Moral Philosophy and the Theory of Education; further, as health is no insignificant means for attaining our end, we must also include the whole science of Medicine, and, as many difficult things are by contrivance rendered easy, and we can in this way gain much time and convenience, the science of Mechanics must in no way be despised. But, before all things, a means must be devised for improving the understanding and purifying it, as far as may be at the outset, so that it may apprehend things without error, and in the best possible way.

Thus it is apparent to everyone that I wish to direct all sciences to one end and aim, so that we may attain to the supreme human perfection which we have named; and, therefore, whatsoever in the sciences does not serve to promote our object will have to be rejected as useless. To sum up the matter in a word, all our actions and thoughts must be directed to this one end. Yet, as it is necessary that while we are endeavouring to attain our purpose, and bring the understanding into the right path, we should carry on our life, we are compelled first of all to lay down certain rules of life as provisionally good, to wit the following:—

I.

To speak in a manner intelligible to the multitude, and to comply with every general custom that does not hinder the attainment of our purpose. For we can gain from the multitude no small advantages, provided that we strive to accommodate ourselves to its understanding as far as possible: moreover, we shall in this way gain a friendly audience for the reception of the truth.

II.

To indulge ourselves with pleasures only in so far as they are necessary for preserving health

III.

Lastly, to endeavour to obtain only sufficient money or other commodities to enable us to preserve our life and health, and to follow such general customs as are consistent with our purpose.

IMMANUEL KANT

(1724-1804)

"So act as to treat humanity, whether in thine own person or in that of any other, in every case as an end withal, never as means only."

H. J. Paton, American scholar, said about "Fundamental Principles of the Metaphysics of Morals" that it is an "indispensable book for all who profess to think seriously about moral problems. Such an observation almost a century and a half after the death of Immanuel Kant, testifies to the significant place the German philosopher holds in the history of metaphysics and ethics. Because Kant's work is difficult to read, his abstract concepts have been subject to distortion and misrepresentation by both his admirers and detractors.

Three longer works, *Critique of Pure Reason, Critique of Practical Reason,* and *Critique of Judgement,* established Kant's enduring place in philosophy as he attempted to offer explanations about faith, freedom, and immortality. His failure to provide satisfactory conclusions to the questions he raised fades in the face of the contribution he made in forcing the discussion of these human concerns to levels that did not exist before him.

The passage included here points to the challenges that the philosopher's style presents to the reader, but it also contains one of the most famous of his concepts–the categorical imperative.

FUNDAMENTAL PRINCIPLES OF THE METAPHYSIC OF MORALS
IMMANUEL KANT

When I conceive a hypothetical imperative, in general I do not know beforehand what it will contain until I am given the condition. But when I conceive a categorical imperative, I know at once what it contains. For as the imperative contains besides the law only the necessity that the maxims shall conform to this law, while the law contains no conditions restricting it, there remains nothing but the general statement that the maxim of the action should conform to a universal law, and it is this conformity alone that the imperative properly represents as necessary.

There is therefore but one categorical imperative, namely, this: *Act only on that maxim whereby thou canst at the same time will that it should become a universal law.*

Now if all imperatives of duty can be deduced from this one imperative as from their principle, then, although it should remain undecided whether what is called duty is not merely a vain notion, yet at least we shall be able to show what we understand by it and what this notion means.

Since the universality of the law according to which effects are produced constitutes what is properly called nature in the most general sense (as to form)–that is, the existence of things so far as it is determined by general laws–the imperative of duty may be expressed thus: *Act as if the maxim of thy action were to become by thy will a universal law of nature.*

We will now enumerate a few duties, adopting the usual division of them into duties to ourselves and to others, and into perfect and imperfect duties.

1. A man reduced to despair by a series of misfortunes feels wearied of life, but is still so far in possession of his reason that he can ask himself whether it would not be contrary to his duty to himself to take his own life. Now he inquires whether the maxim of his action could become a universal law of nature. His maxim

is: From self-love I adopt it as a principle to shorten my life when its longer duration is likely to bring more evil than satisfaction. It is asked then simply whether this principle founded on self-love can become a universal law of nature. Now we see at once that a system of nature of which it should be a law to destroy life by means of the very feeling whose special nature it is to impel to the improvement of life would contradict itself, and therefore could not exist as a system of nature; hence that maxim cannot possibly exist as a universal law of nature, and consequently would be wholly inconsistent with the supreme principle of all duty.

2. Another finds himself forced by necessity to borrow money. He knows that he will not be able to repay it, but sees also that nothing will be lent to him unless he promises stoutly to repay it in a definite time. He desires to make this promise, but he has still so much conscience as to ask himself: Is it not unlawful and inconsistent with duty to get out of a difficulty in this way? Suppose, however, that he resolves to do so, then the maxim of his action would be expressed thus: When I think myself in want of money, I will borrow money and promise to repay it, although I know that I never can do so. Now this principle of self-love or of one's own advantage may perhaps be consistent with my whole future welfare; but the question now is, Is it right? I change then the suggestion of self-love into a universal law, and state the question thus: How would it be if my maxim were a universal law? Then I see at once that it could never hold as a universal law of nature, but would necessarily contradict itself. For supposing it to be a universal law that everyone when he thinks himself in a difficulty should be able to promise whatever he pleases with the purpose of not keeping his promise, the promise itself would become impossible, as well as the end that one might have in view of it, since no one would consider that anything was promised to him, but would ridicule all such statements as vain pretenses.

3. A third finds himself a talent which with the help of some culture might make him a useful man in many respects. But he finds himself in comfortable circumstances and prefers to indulge in pleasure rather than to take pains in enlarging and

improving his happy natural capacities. He asks, however, whether his maxim of neglect of his natural gifts, besides agreeing with his inclination to indulgence, agrees also with what is called duty. He sees then that a system of nature could indeed subsist with such a universal law, although men (like the South Sea islanders) should let their talents rest and resolve to devote their lives merely to idleness, amusement, and propagation of their species–in a word, to enjoyment; but he cannot possibly *will* that this should be a universal law of nature, or be implanted in us as such by a natural instinct. For, as a rational being, he necessarily wills that his faculties be developed, since they serve him, and have been given him, for all sorts of possible purposes.

4. A fourth, who is in prosperity, while he sees that others have to contend with great wretchedness and that he could help them, thinks: What concern is it of mine? Let everyone be as happy as Heaven pleases, or as he can make himself; I will take nothing from him nor even envy him, only I do not wish to contribute anything to his welfare or to his assistance in distress! Now no doubt, if such a mode of thinking were a universal law, the human race might very well subsist, and doubtless even better than in a state in which everyone talks of sympathy and goodwill, or even takes care occasionally to put it into practice, but, on the other side, also cheats when he can, betrays the rights of men, or otherwise violates them. But although it is possible that a universal law of nature might exist in accordance with that maxim, it is impossible to will that such a principle should have the universal validity of a law of nature. For a will which resolved this would contradict itself, inasmuch as many cases might occur in which one would have need of the love and sympathy of others, and in which, by such a law of nature, sprung from his own will, he would deprive himself of all hope of the aid he desires.

These are a few of the many actual duties, or at least what we regard as such, which obviously fall into two classes on the one principle that we have laid down. We must be *able to will* that a maxim of our action should be a universal law. This is the canon of the moral appreciation of the action generally. Some actions are of such a character that their maxim cannot without contradiction be even *conceived* as a universal law of nature, far from it being possible that we should *will* that it *should* be so. In others, this intrinsic impossibility is not found, but still it is impossible to *will* that their maxim should be raised to the universality of a law of nature, since such a will would contradict itself. It is easily seen that the former violate strict or rigorous (inflexible) duty; the latter only laxer (meritorious) duty. Thus it has been completely shown by these examples how all duties depend as regards the nature of the obligation (not the object of the action) on the same principle.

The question then is this: Is it a necessary law *for all rational beings* that they should always judge of their actions by maxims of which they can themselves will that they should serve as universal laws? If it is so, then it must be connected (altogether a *priori*) with the very conception of the will of a rational being generally. But in order to discover this connection we must, however reluctantly, take a step into metaphysic, although into a domain of it which is distinct from speculative philosophy–namely, the metaphysic of morals. In a practical philosophy, where it is not the reasons of what *happens* that we have to ascertain, but the laws of what *ought to happen,* even although it never does, that is, objective practical laws, there it is not necessary to inquire into the reasons why anything pleases or displeases, how the pleasure of mere sensation differs from taste, and whether the latter is distinct from a general satisfaction of reason; on what the feeling of pleasure or pain rests, and how from it desires and inclinations arise, and from these again maxims by the cooperation of reason; for all this belongs to an empirical psychology, which would constitute the second part of physics, if we regard physics as the philosophy of nature, so far as it is based on *empirical laws*. But here we are concerned with objective practical laws, and consequently with the relation of the will to itself so far as it is determined by reason alone, in which case whatever has reference to anything empirical is necessarily excluded; since if *reason of itself alone* determines the conduct (and it is the possibility of this that we are now investigating), it must necessarily do so *a priori*.

The will is conceived as a faculty of determining oneself to action *in accordance with the conception of certain laws.* And such a faculty can be found only in rational beings. Now that which serves the will as the objective ground of its self-determination is the *end*, and if this is assigned by reason alone, it must hold for all rational beings. On the other hand, that which merely contains the ground of possibility of the action of which the effect is the end, this is called the *means*. The subjective ground of the desire is the *spring,* the objective ground of the volition is the *motive;* hence the distinction between subjective ends which rest on springs, and objective ends which depend on motives valid for every rational being. Practical principles are *formal* when they abstract from all subjective ends; they are *material* when they assume these, and therefore particular, springs of action. The ends which a rational being proposes to himself at pleasure as *effects* of his actions (material ends) are all only relative, for it is only their relation to the particular desires of the subject that gives them their worth, which therefore cannot furnish principles universal and necessary for all rational beings and for every volition, that is to say, practical laws. Hence all these relative ends can give rise only to hypothetical imperatives.

Supposing, however, that there were something *whose existence* has *in itself* an absolute worth, something which, being *an end in itself,* could be a source of definite laws, then in this and this alone would lie the source of a possible categorical imperative, that is, a practical law.

Now I say: man and generally any rational being *exists* as an end in himself, *not merely as a means* to be arbitrarily used by this or that will, but in all his actions, whether they concern himself or other rational beings, must be always regarded at the same time as an end. All objects of the inclinations have only a conditional worth; for if the inclinations and the wants founded on them did not exist, then their object would be without value. But the inclinations themselves, being sources of want, are so far from having an absolute worth for which they should be desired that, on the contrary, it must be the universal wish of every rational being to be wholly free from them. Thus the worth of any object which is *to be acquired* by our action is always conditional. Beings whose existence depends not on our will but on Nature's, have nevertheless, if they are nonrational beings, only a relative value as means, and are therefore called *things*; rational beings, on the contrary, are called *persons*, because their very nature points them out as ends in themselves, that is, as something which must not be used merely as means, and so far therefore restricts freedom of action (and is an object of respect). These, therefore, are not merely subjective ends whose existence has a worth *for us* as an effect of our action, but *objective ends,* that is, things whose existence is an end in itself–an end, moreover, for which no other can be substituted, which they should subserve *merely* as means, for otherwise nothing whatever would *possess absolute* worth; but if all worth were conditioned and therefore contingent, then there would be no supreme practical principle of reason whatever.

If then there is a supreme practical principle or, in respect of the human will, a categorical imperative, it must be one which, being drawn from the conception of that which is necessarily an end for everyone because it is *an end in itself*, constitutes an *objective* principle of will, and can therefore serve as a universal practical law. The foundation of this principle is: *rational nature exists as an end in itself.* Man necessarily conceives his own existence as being so; so far then this is a *subjective* principle of human actions. But every other rational being regards its existence similarly, just on the same rational principle that holds for me; so that it is at the same time an objective principle from which as a supreme practical law all laws of the will must be capable of being deduced. Accordingly the practical imperative will be as follows: *So act as to treat humanity, whether in thine own person or in that of any other, in every case as an end withal, never as means only.* We will now inquire whether this can be practically carried out.

To abide by the previous examples:

First, under the head of necessary duty to oneself: He who contemplates suicide should ask himself whether his action can be consistent with the idea of humanity *as an end in itself.* If he destroys himself in order to escape from painful circumstances, he uses a person merely as *a mean* to maintain a tolerable condition up to the end of life. But a man is not a thing, that is to say, something which can be used merely as means, but must in all his actions be always considered as an end in himself. I cannot, therefore, dispose in any way of a man in my own person so as to mutilate him, to damage or kill him. (It belongs to ethics proper to define this principle more precisely, so as to avoid all misunderstanding, for example, as to the amputation of the limbs in order to preserve myself; as to exposing my life to danger with a view to preserve it, etc. This question is therefore omitted here.)

Secondly, as regards necessary duties, or those of strict obligation, towards others: He who is thinking of making a lying promise to others will see at once that he would be using another man *merely as a mean,* without the latter containing at the same time the end in himself. For he whom I propose by such a promise to use for my own purposes cannot possible assent to my mode of acting towards him, and therefore cannot himself contain the end of this action. This violation of the principles of humanity in other men is more obvious if we take in examples of attacks on the freedom and property of others. For then it is clear that he who transgresses the rights of men intends to use the person of others merely as means, without considering that as rational beings they ought always to be esteemed also as ends, that is, as beings who must be capable of containing in themselves the end of the very same action.

Thirdly, as regards contingent (meritorious) duties to oneself: It is not enough that the action does not violate humanity in our own person as an end in itself, it must also *harmonize with* it. Now there are in humanity capacities of greater perfection which belong to the end that nature has in view in regard to humanity in ourselves as the subject; to neglect these might perhaps be consistent with the *maintenance* of humanity as an end in itself, but not with the *advancement* of this end.

Fourthly, as regards meritorious duties towards others: The natural end which all men have is their own happiness. Now humanity might indeed subsist although no one should contribute anything to the happiness of others, provided he did not intentionally withdraw anything from it; but after all, this would only harmonize negatively, not positively, with *humanity as an end in itself,* if everyone does not also endeavor, as far as in him lies, to forward the ends of others. For the ends of any subject which is an end in himself ought as far as possible to be *my* ends also, if that conception is to have its *full* effect with me.

BARON DE MONTESQUIEU

(1689-1755)

"But constant experience shows us that every man invested with power is apt to abuse it, and to carry his authority as far as it will go."

Charles Louis de Secondat (The Baron de Montesquieu) was born in Bordeaux, France, in 1689. He came from a wealthy family and upon the death of his father in 1717 was placed under the care of his uncle, Baron de Montesquieu. Upon his uncle's death he inherited the title of Baron de Montesquieu. Montesquieu was trained as a lawyer and took a great interest in the study of governments. He was also fascinated with the customs of peoples and would later develop much of his political theory on the idea that climates and customs somewhat dictate the type of government suitable to a particular region.

In 1721 Montesquieu published his work *Persian Letters*, which brought to the attention of the reading public the abuses of the French nobility and the church. Although his work was controversial, he was able to avoid serious repercussions because of his rank and privilege. In 1748 Montesquieu published his most important work *On the Spirit of the Laws*. This work organized Montesquieu's ideas on government and explains the best type of government needed to check the vested interests of mankind.

Montesquieu in his *Spirit of the Laws* identifies three types of governments: a monarchy, a republic, and despotism. Montesquieu clearly favors a republic as a superior form of government. He was influenced by the English model of government, which he saw as "balanced" by a king, an elected parliament, and a developed court system. This "balance of powers" according to Montesquieu, would keep the greed of men in check. If the powers of government are divided among three branches: the executive (king), the legislative (parliament), and the judicial (court system), no individual or group can dominate.

The concept of separation of powers greatly influenced the founding fathers of the United States. They read Montesquieu thoroughly and sought to incorporate his ideas into the American Constitution. Two hundred plus years after its ratification, *The United States Constitution* continues to operate under the basic principles outlined by Montesquieu in 1748.

(The Enlightenment concerned itself with many ideas, including government. Montesquieu's The Spirit of the Laws, written in 1748, was the most influential political work of the Enlightenment.)

Montesquieu's Spirit of the Laws (1748)

Democratic and aristocratic states are not in their own nature free. Political liberty is to be found only in moderate governments; and even in these it is not always found. It is there only when there is no abuse of power. But constant experience shows us that every man invested with power is apt to abuse it, and to carry his authority as far as it will go....

To prevent this abuse, it is necessary from the very nature of things that power should be a check to power....

In every government there are three sorts of power: the legislative; the executive in respect to things dependent on the law of nations; and the executive in regard to matters that depend on the civil law [the realm of the judiciary]....

The political liberty of the subject is a tranquility of mind arising from the opinion each person has of his safety. In order to have this liberty, it is requisite that government be so constituted as one man need not be afraid of another.

When the legislative and executive powers are united in the same person, or in the same body of magistrates, there can be no liberty; because apprehensions may arise, lest the same monarch or senate should enact tyrannical laws, to execute them in a tyrannical manner.

Again, there is no liberty, if the judiciary power be not separated from the legislative and executive. Were it joined with the legislative, the life and liberty of the subject would be exposed to arbitrary control; for the judge would be then the legislator. Were it joined to the executive power, the judge might behave with violence and oppression.

There would be an end of everything, were the same man or the same body, whether of the nobles or of the people, to exercise those three powers, that of enacting laws, that of executing the public resolutions, and of trying the causes of individuals. (From Montesquieu's *Spirit of the Laws*, 1748)

VOLTAIRE

(1694-1778)

"What can we say to a man who tells you that he would rather obey God than men, and that therefore he is sure to go to heaven for butchering you?"

Francois Marie Arouet, who later took the pen name of Voltaire, was born in Paris, 1694. The son of a minor government official, Voltaire received an excellent education under the Jesuits at the College Louis-le-Grand. Voltaire was primarily interested in literature, philosophy, and writing. He earned a reputation for possessing a biting wit and wrote a number of satires lampooning the upper classes. One of his works, a satire of the duc' d'Orleans, landed him in the notorious Bastille. Another quarrel erupted with the chevalier de Rohan at a dinner party when Rohan made light of Voltaire's name. Voltaire, ever quick to respond, told Rohan, "at least I give honor to my name." A second trip to the Bastille resulted.

After his second imprisonment, Voltaire was released with the agreement he would exile himself to England. Voltaire's time in England between 1725 and 1728, was a productive time. Voltaire was impressed with the relative freedom afforded the English people and the respect the English gave to learned men, in particular, the ornate funeral given to Sir Isaac Newton. By 1728 Voltaire was back in France writing novels, plays, short stories, and continuing his satirical works on French society. His open attacks on the French church put him on the run once again. He continually pointed out the intolerance of the church, which he summarized in his famous phrase 'ecrasons l'infame" (crush the infamous thing).

Despite his scrapes with French authorities, Voltaire was extremely popular and was the most widely read of the French philosophers. An ardent player of the markets, Voltaire made a fortune speculating in the stock markets of Europe. Despite his railings against the aristocracy and the intolerance of the Catholic

Church, Voltaire seemed quite at home with the privileged classes. While his most famous works, such as *Candide* written in 1759, continued to make great use of satire at the expense of the privileged few, Voltaire apparently felt no qualms about enjoying many of those privileges for himself. Voltaire, however, can be said to have developed the modern form of criticism. His satirical style and his willingness to offend mark him as a man of courage. During the French Revolution, the bodies of Rousseau and Voltaire were brought to Paris for special burials within the Pantheon. Voltaire had become the symbol of French rationalist thought.

(Voltaire was by far the most widely read of the Enlightenment figures. He was immensely popular. Voltaire wrote on a variety of subjects, including religion and government.)

Voltaire on Religion (1764)

Fanaticism is to superstition what delirium is to fever and rage to anger. The man visited by ecstasies and visions, who takes dreams from realities and his fancies for prophecies, is an enthusiast; the man who supports his madness with murder is a fanatic....

The most detestable example of fanaticism was that of the burghers of Paris who on St. Bartholomew's Night [1572] went about assassinating and butchering all their fellow citizens who did not go to mass, throwing them out of the windows, cutting them to pieces.

Once fanaticism has corrupted a mind, the malady is almost incurable....

The only remedy for this epidemic malady is the philosophical spirit which, spread gradually, at last tames men's habits and prevents the disease from starting; for once the disease has made any progress, one must flee and wait for the air to clear itself. Laws and religion are not strong enough against the spiritual pest; religion, far from being healthy food for infected brains, turns to poison in them....

Even the law is impotent against these attacks of rage; it is like reading a court decree to a raving maniac. These fellows are certain that the holy spirit with which they are filled is above the law, that their enthusiasm is the only law they must obey.

What can we say to a man who tells you that he would rather obey God than men, and that therefore he is sure to go to heaven for butchering you?

Ordinarily fanatics are guided by rascals, who put the dagger into their hands; these latter resemble that Old Man of the Mountain who is supposed to have made imbeciles taste the joys of paradise and who promised them an eternity of the pleasures of which he had given them a foretaste, on condition that they assassinated all those he would name to them. There is only one religion in the world that has never been sullied by fanaticism, that of the Chinese men of letters. The schools of philosophy were not only free from this pest, they were its remedy; for the effect of philosophy is to make the soul tranquil, and fanaticism is incompatible with tranquility. If our holy religions have so often been corrupted by this infernal delirium, it is the madness of men which is at fault.

(From Voltaire's *Philosophical Dictionary,* 1764)

Voltaire's Support of Enlightened Despotism

1. We are intelligent beings, and intelligent creatures cannot have been created by a blind and unfeeling beast; there are certainly some differences between the ideas of a Newton and the braying of a mule. The intelligence of Newton springs, therefore, from another [higher] intelligence.

   When we see a fine mechanism, we say that it was created by a good mechanic, and that that mechanic has a good understanding of such matters. The world is surely an admirable machine: therefore there must exist in this globe a wonderful intelligence, whatsoever it may be. This argument is not the worse for being old.

   The movements of the stars, those of our little earth moving around the sun, all operate according to profound *mathematical* laws. Did not even Plato, who did not know one of these laws, the eloquent but mistaken Plato...who was even ignorant of the trigonometry of spheres, nevertheless have a genius good enough, and an instinct happy enough to call God the eternal geometrician; thus sensing that there exists a formative intelligence in the universe?...It is impossible to dispute this truth, which surrounds us and presses in upon us from all sides....

2. It is impossible that there were ever on earth a state whose government was not, at first, that of a republic, for that is the natural working of human nature. Some families unite at first, against the bear and the wolf; he who has grain furnishes it in exchange for wood.

   When we discovered America, we found all the people divided into republics, there were only two monarchies in that part of the world. Of [a] thousand nations we found only two oppressed.

   And now what is better, that our fatherland should be a republican or a monarchial state? For four thousand years one has debated this question. Ask the rich for the solution, and they will love an aristocracy best, ask the people and they prefer a democracy; only the kings prefer a monarchy. How then is it possible that almost the whole globe is governed by monarchs?...But, truly, the real reason is, as has been said, that men are very rarely worthy to govern themselves.... Equality, the natural birthright of men, exists still among the Swiss to the extent to which it is possible. By that word you must not understand that absurd and impossible equality by means of which the servant and the master...the plaintiff and the judge are confounded with one another. But that equality instead by which the citizen only depends on the laws which protect the freedom of the feeble against the ambitions of the strong.

JEAN JACQUES ROUSSEAU

(1712-1788)

"Man is born free, and yet is everywhere in fetters."

Jean Jacques Rousseau was born in Geneva, Switzerland. Following a troubled youth, Rousseau took up residence in Paris. After winning an important essay contest in which he railed against the progress of the sciences, Rousseau became a well known writer and philosopher. In contrast to the mainstream of the Enlightenment, Rousseau was a proponent of emotion and nature as truer and more reliable than reason alone. Nature, according to Rousseau, held the key to leading a good life. Only a natural life could allow mankind to live in peace and harmony with his fellow men, and with himself. Rousseau's works would have a profound influence on philosophy, the arts, and on political theory.

The Social Contract is perhaps Rousseau's most enduring and influential work. Like Hobbes, Rousseau recognized the need for mankind to create political units. Unlike Hobbes, Rousseau saw mankind as essentially good. But mankind has strayed so far from nature that he cannot return to its unspoiled simplicity. He must now form social contracts to ensure his freedom. The controversy surrounding *The Social Contract* is substantial. While Rousseau seems to imply that the social contract can only come about through the agreement of the people, he leaves us somewhat in doubt as to how the contract is to be formed. He speaks of a General Will of the people. But how is the General Will to be discerned?

Because of the vagueness of Rousseau's *The Social Contract*, it has alternatively been cited by advocates of democratic states, dictatorships, and virtually every other type of government, as supporting their particular theory. Indeed, Karl Marx used portions of *The Social Contract* in his *Communist Manifesto*. Rousseau died a year before the onset of the French Revolution, but his writings, especially *The Social Contract*, would have a substantial impact on the revolution.

THE SOCIAL CONTRACT
JEAN JACQUES ROUSSEAU

I-The Terms of the Compact

My object is to discover whether in civil polity there is any legitimate and definite canon of government, taking men as they are and laws as they might be. In this inquiry I shall uniformly try to reconcile that which is permitted by right with that which is prescribed by interest so as to avoid the clash of justice with utility.

Man is born free, and yet is everywhere in fetters. He is governed, obliged to obey laws. What is it that legitimises this subjection to government? I think I can solve the problem.

It is not merely a matter of force; force is only the power of the strongest and must yield when a greater strength arises; there is here no question of right, but simply of might. But social order is a sacred right that serves as a base to all others. This right, however, does not come from nature; it is founded upon conventions.

The explanation of social order is not to be found in the family tie, since when a child grows up it escapes from tutelage; the parent's right to exercise authority is only temporary. Nor can government be based on servitude. An individual man may sell his liberty to another for sustenance; but a nation cannot sell its liberty—it does not receive sustenance from its ruler but, on the contrary, sustains him. The gift is a civil act which presupposes a public deliberation. Before, then, we examine the act by which a people chooses a king, it would be well to examine the act by which a people becomes a people.

Let it be assumed that the obstacles which prejudice the conversation of man in the state of nature have prevailed by their resistance over the forces which each individual is able to employ to keep himself in that state. The primitive condition can then no longer exist; mankind must change it or perish.

The problem with which men are confronted in these circumstances may be stated as follows: "to find a form of association that defends and protects with all the common force the person and property of each partner, and by which each partner, uniting himself with all the rest, nevertheless obeys only himself, and remains as free as heretofore." To this problem the social contract affords a solution.

The essence of the pact is the total and unreserved alienation by each partner of all his rights to the community as a whole. No individual can retain any rights that are not possessed equally by all other individuals without the compact being thereby violated. Again, each partner, by yielding his rights to the community, yields them to no individual, and thus in his relations with individuals he regains all the rights he has sacrificed.

The compact, therefore, may be reduced to the following terms: 'Each of us places in common his person and all his power under the supreme direction of the general will, and we receive each member as an indivisible part of the whole.'

By this act is created a moral and collective body, composed of as many members as the society has voices, receiving from this same act its unity, its common "I," its life and its will. This body is the republic, called by its members the state when passive, the sovereign when active. The partners are collectively called the people; they are citizens, as participants in the sovereign authority, and subjects, as under obligations to the laws of the state.

By passing through the compact, from the state of nature to the civil state man substitutes justice for instinct in his conduct and gives to his actions a morality of which they were formerly devoid. What man loses by the contract is his natural liberty and an illimitable right to all that tempts him and that he can obtain; what he gains is civil liberty and a right of secure property in all that he possesses.

I shall conclude this chapter with a remark which should serve as a basis for the whole social system. It is that in place of destroying natural liberty, the fundamental pact substitutes a moral and legitimate equality for the natural physical inequality between men, and that, while men may be unequal in strength and talent, they are all made equal by convention and right.

II-The Sovereign and the Laws

The first and most important consequence of the principles above established is that only the general will can direct the forces of the state towards the aim of its institution, which is the common good; for if the antagonism of particular interests has rendered necessary the establishment of political societies, it is the accord of these interests that has rendered such societies possible.

I maintain, then, that sovereignty, being the exercise of the general will, cannot be alienated and that the sovereign, which is simply a collective being, cannot be represented save by itself; it may transfer its power, but not its will.

For the same reason that sovereignty is inalienable it is indivisible. For the will is either general, or it is not. If it is general, it is, when declared, an act of the people and becomes law; if it is not general, it is, when declared, merely an act of a particular person or persons, not of the sovereign.

A law is an expression of the general will and must be general in its terms and import. The sovereign cannot legislate for part of the individuals composing a state, for if it did so the general will would enter into a particular relation with particular people, and that is contrary to its nature. The law may thus confer privileges, but must not name the persons to whom the privileges are to belong; it may establish a royal government, but must not nominate a king. Any function relating to an individual object does not appertain to the legislative power.

As a popular assembly is not always enlightened in its judgements–though the general will, when properly ascertained, must be right–the service of a wise legislator is necessary to draw up laws for the sovereign's approval.

The legislator, if he be truly wise, will not begin by writing down laws that are good in the abstract, but will first look about to see whether the people for whom he intends them is capable of upholding them. He must bear in mind many considerations–the situation of the country, the nature of the soil, the density of the population, the national history, occupations and aptitudes.

Among these considerations one of the most important is the area of the state. As nature has given limits to the stature of a normal man, beyond which she makes only giants or dwarfs, there are also limits beyond which a state is, in the one direction, too large to be well governed, and, in the other too small to maintain itself. There is in every body politic a maximum of force which cannot be exceeded, and from which the state often falls away by the process of enlarging itself. The further the social bond is extended, the slacker it becomes; and, in general, a small state is proportionately stronger than a large one.

It is true that a state must have a certain breadth of base for the sake of solidity and in order to resist violent shocks from without. But, on the other hand, administration becomes more troublesome with distance. It increases in burdensomeness, moreover, with the multiplication of degrees. Each town, district and province has its administration, for which the people must pay. Finally, overwhelming everything, is the remote central administration.

Again, the government in a large state has less vigour and swiftness than in a small one; the people have less affection for their chiefs, for their country and for each other–since they are, for the most part, strangers to each other. Uniform laws are not suitable for diverse provinces; yet diverse laws among people belonging to the same state breed weakness and confusion.

The greatest good of all, which should be the aim of every system of legislation, may on investigation be reduced to two main objects–*liberty* and *equality*: liberty, because all dependence of individuals on other individuals is so much force taken away from the body of the state; equality, because without it liberty cannot exist.

III-The Government

Every free action has two causes which concur to produce it; one of them the will that determines upon the act, the other the power that performs it. In the political body one must distinguish between these two–the legislative power and the executive power. The executive power cannot belong to the sovereign, inasmuch as executive acts are particular acts, aimed at individuals, and therefore, as already explained, outside the sovereign's sphere. Public force, then, requires an agent to apply it according to the direction of the general will.

This is the government, erroneously confounded with the sovereign, of which it is only the minister. It is an intermediary body established between subjects and sovereign for their mutual correspondence, for the execution of the laws and the maintenance of civil and political liberty.

The magistrates who form the government may be numerous, or may be few; and, generally speaking, the fewer the magistrates the stronger the government. A magistrate has three wills– his personal will, his will as one of the governors and his will as a member of the sovereign. The last-named is the weakest, the first-named the most powerful.

If there is only one governor, the two stronger wills are concentrated in one man; with a few governors, they are concentrated in few men; when the government is in the hands of all the citizens, the second will be obliterated and the first widely distributed, and the government is consequently weak.

On the other hand, where there are many governors the government will be more readily kept in correspondence with the general will. The duty of the legislator is to hit the happy medium at which the government, while not failing in strength, is yet properly submissive to the sovereign.

The sovereign may, in the first place, entrust the government to the whole people or the greater part of them; this form is called democracy. Or it may be placed in the hands of a minority, in which case it is called aristocracy. Or it may be concentrated in the hands of a single magistrate from whom all the others derive their power; this is called monarchy.

It may be urged, on behalf of democracy, that those who make the laws know better than anybody how they should be interpreted and administered. But it is not right that the makers of the laws should execute them, nor that the main body of the people should turn its attention from general views to particular objects. Nothing is more dangerous than the influence of private interests on public affairs. A true democracy, in the vigorous sense of the term, never has existed and never will. It is against nature that the many should govern and the few be governed. A people composed of gods would govern itself democratically.

There are three forms of aristocracy–natural, elective and

hereditary. The first is only adapted to simple peoples; the third is the worst of all governments; the second is the best of all. By the elective method, probity, sagacity and experience afford guarantees that the community will be wisely governed.

The first defect of monarchy is that it is to the interest of the monarch to keep the people in a state of weakness and misery, so that they may be unable to resist his power. Another is that under a monarchy the posts of honour are occupied by bunglers and rascals who win their promotion by petty court intrigue. Again, an elective monarchy is a cause of disorder whenever a king dies; and a hereditary monarchy leaves the character of the king to chance, which generally goes astray.

Since the sovereign has no power except its legislative authority, it only acts by laws; and since the laws are simply the authentic acts of the general will, the sovereign cannot act save when the people are assembled. It is essential that there should be definitely fixed periodic assemblies of the people that cannot be abolished or delayed, so that on the appointed day the people will be legitimately convoked by the law.

But between the sovereign authority and arbitrary government there is sometimes introduced a middle power, of which I ought to speak. As soon as the public services cease to be the main interest of the citizens, as soon as they prefer to serve their purses rather than themselves, the state is nearing its ruin. The weakening of patriotism, the activity of private interests, the immensity of states, conquests, and the abuse of government have led to the device of deputies or representatives of the people in the national assemblies. But sovereignty cannot be represented, even as it cannot be alienated; it consists essentially in the general will, and the will is not ascertainable by representation; it is either itself, or something else; there is no middle course. A law not ratified by the people in person is no law at all. The English people believes itself free, but it greatly deceives itself; it is not so, except during the election of members of parliament. As soon as they are elected, it is enslaved.

How are we to conceive the act by which the government is instituted? The first process is the determination of the sovereign that the government shall assume such and such a form; this is the establishment of a law. The second process is the nomination by the people of those to whom the government is to be entrusted; this is not a law, but a function of government.

It is a logical sequence of the social contract that in the assemblies of the people the voice of the majority prevails. The only law requiring unanimity is the contract itself. But how can a man be free, and at the same time submit to laws to which he has not consented?

I reply that when a law is proposed in the popular assembly the question put is not precisely whether the citizens approve or disapprove of it, but whether it conforms or not to the general will. The minority, then, simply have it proved to them that they estimated the general will wrongly. Once it is declared, they are, as citizens, participants in it, and as subjects they must obey it.

ADAM SMITH

(1723-1790)

"It is not to the benevolence of the butcher or the baker that we owe our daily bread, but to their own self interest."

Adam Smith was born in Kirkaldy, Scotland, in 1723. He was educated at the universities of Glasgow and Oxford where he took a great interest in rhetoric and philosophy. During his university days Smith developed a life-long friendship with the philosopher David Hume. Hume would have a substantial influence on Smith's ethical and economic philosophy. Smith obtained the title of professor of moral philosophy at the University of Glasgow, a post he held until his resignation in 1763. In 1763 Smith traveled to France where he came under the influence of Francois Quesnay, the leader of a group of philosophers known as the Physiocrats. The Physiocrats promoted the idea of laissez-faire, the concept that government should play a limited role in the economy. This viewpoint stood in direct contrast to the prevailing economic theory of mercantilism.

Smith developed the concept of laissez-faire into a full economic treatise, which he published under the title *Inquiry into the Nature and Causes of the Wealth of Nations*, generally referred to by the shortened title *Wealth of Nations*. In this work Smith maintains that labor, rather than agriculture, is the true source of wealth. Moreover, he maintains that each individual should be allowed to pursue his own interest(s) with a minimum of government intervention. The state could intervene for the settlement of disputes, to develop certain public utilities, to promote public health, but for little else. Smith's laissez-faire doctrine would have a significant influence on eighteenth century industrialists, who saw in Smith's work a tailor-made rationale for their individual pursuits.

Perhaps Smith's greatest influence was on the economic system of the United States. *The Wealth of Nations*, as noted, was published in 1776 just as the colonies were declaring their independence from England. The Americans saw in Smith's work the personification of the philosophy of individual rights, which they were using as the justification for their revolution.

(In his famous Wealth of Nations, *Adam Smith discusses the legitimate role for government in a laissez-faire economy.)*

Wealth of Nations

...According to the system of natural liberty, the sovereign has only three duties to attend to; three duties of great importance, indeed, but plain and intelligible to common understandings: first, the duty of protecting the society from the violence and invasion of other independent societies; secondly, the duty of protecting, as far as possible, every member of the society from the injustice or oppression of every other member of it, or the duty of establishing an exact administration of justice; and, thirdly, the duty of erecting and maintaining certain public works and certain public institutions, which it can never be for the interest of any individual, or small number of individuals, to erect and maintain; because the profit could never repay the expense to any individual or small number of individuals, though it may frequently do much more than repay it to a great society.

Adam Smith, *An Inquiry into the Nature and Causes of the Wealth of Nations*, ed. Edwin Cannan (New York: Random House, 1937), p. 651. (Reprinted by permission of the publisher.)

PART FOUR

(In 1789, members of the Third Estate presented Louis XVI with a list of grievances. Note the demands for equality contained in these "cashiers.")

Demands of the Third Estate in 1789

The order of the third estate of the City...of Dourdan...supplicates [the king] to accept the grievances, complaints, and remonstrances which it is permitted to bring to the foot of the throne, and to see therein only the expression of its zeal and the homage of its obedience.
It wishes:
1. That his subjects of the third estate, equal by such status to all other citizens, present themselves before the common father without other distinction which might degrade them.
2. That all the orders, already united by duty and a common desire to contribute equally to the needs of the State, also deliberate in common concerning its needs.
3. That no citizen lose his liberty except according to law; that, consequently, no one be arrested by virtue of special orders, or, if imperative circumstances necessitate such orders, that the prisoner be handed over to regular courts of justice within forty-eight hours at the latest.

......

12. That every tax, direct or indirect, be granted only for a limited time, and that every collection beyond such term be regarded as peculation, and punished by such.

......

15. That every personal tax be abolished; that thus the capitation {a poll tax} and the taille {tax from which nobility and clergy were exempt} and its accessories be merged with the vingtiémes {an income tax} in a tax on land and real or nominal property.

16. That such tax be borne equally, without distinction, by all classes of citizens and by all kinds of property, even feudal...rights.
17. That the tax substituted for the corvée be borne by all classes of citizens equally and without distinction. That said tax, at present beyond the capacity of those who pay it and the needs to which it is destined, be reduced by at least one-half.

On August 27, 1789, the National Assembly approved a document entitled The Declaration of the Rights of Man and Citizen. *The document is modeled after the American Declaration of Independence.)*

The Declaration of the Rights of Man and Citizen (1789)

The representatives of the French people, organized as a National Assembly, believing that the ignorance, neglect or contempt of the rights of man are the sole cause of public calamities and of the corruption of the governments, have determined to set forth in a solemn declaration the natural, inalienable and sacred rights of man, in order that this declaration, being constantly before all the members of the social body, shall remind them continually of their rights and duties; in order that the acts of the legislative power, as well as those of the executive power, may be compared at any moment with the ends of all political institutions and may thus be more respected; and, lastly in order that the grievances of the citizens, based hereafter upon simple and incontestable principles, shall tend to the maintenance of the constitution and redound to the happiness of all. Therefore the National Assembly recognizes and proclaims, in the presence and under the auspices of the Supreme Being, the following rights of man and of the citizens:—

ARTICLE

1. Men are born and remain free and equal in rights. Social distinctions may only be founded upon the general good.
2. The aim of all political association is the preservation of the natural and imprescriptible rights of man. These rights are liberty, property, security and resistance to oppression.
3. The principle of all sovereignty resides essentially in the nation. No body nor individual may exercise any authority which does not proceed directly from the nation.

4. Liberty consists in the freedom to do everything which injures no one else; hence the exercise of the natural rights of each man has no limits except those which assure to the other members of the society the enjoyment of the same rights. These limits can only be determined by law.
5. Law can only prohibit such actions as are hurtful to society. Nothing may be prevented which is not forbidden by law, and no one may be forced to do anything not provided for by law.
6. Law is the expression of the general will. Every citizen has a right to participate personally or through his representative in its formation. It must be the same for all, whether it protects or punishes. All citizens, being equal in the eyes of the law, are equally eligible to all dignities and to all public positions and occupations, according to their abilities, and without distinction except that of their virtues and talents.
7. No person shall be accused, arrested or imprisoned except in the cases and according to the forms prescribed by law. Any one soliciting, transmitting, executing or causing to be executed any arbitrary order shall be punished. But any citizen summoned or arrested in virtue of the law shall submit without delay, as resistance constitutes an offence.
8. The law shall provide for such punishments only as are strictly and obviously necessary, and no one shall suffer punishment except it be legally inflicted in virtue of a law passed and promulgated before the commission of the offence.
9. As all persons are held innocent until they shall have been declared guilty, if arrest shall be deemed indispensable, all harshness not essential to the securing of the prisoner's person shall be severely repressed by law.
10. No one shall be disquieted on account of his opinions, including his religious views, provided their manifestation does not disturb the public order established by law.
11. The free communication of ideas and opinions is one of the most precious of the rights of man. Every citizen may, accordingly, speak, write and print with freedom, but shall be responsible for such abuses of this freedom as shall be defined by law.

12. The security of the rights of man and of the citizen requires public military force. These forces are, therefore, established for the good of all and not for the personal advantage of those to whom they shall be entrusted.
13. A common contribution is essential for the maintenance of the public forces and for the cost of administration. This should be equitably distributed among all the citizens in proportion to their means.
14. All citizens have a right to decide, either personally or by their representatives, as to the necessity of the public contribution; to grant this freely; to know to what uses it is put; and to fix the proportion, the mode of assessment, and of collection, and the duration of the taxes.
15. Society has the right to require of every public agent an account of his administration.
16. A society in which the observance of the law is not assured, nor the separation of powers defined, has no constitution at all.
17. Since property is an inviolable and sacred right, no one shall be deprived thereof except where public necessity, legally determined, shall clearly demand it, and then only on condition that the owner shall have been previously and equitably indemnified.

(From the *Declaration of Rights of Man and Citizen*, 1789)

EDMUND BURKE

(1729-1797)

"The improvements of the National Assembly are superficial, their errors fundamental."

Edmund Burke was born in Dublin, Ireland, in 1729. He studied law at Trinity College in Ireland but gave up the study of law to embark on a literary career, earning a reputation as a political satirist. In 1756 he published a work entitled *Vindication of Natural Society* in which he lampooned the political philosophy of Henry Bolingbroke, an influential English politician. In addition to his political satires, Burke wrote numerous articles for the *Annual Register*, a widely read British periodical.

In 1766 Burke was elected to the House of Commons via the Whig party. He quickly earned a reputation as a spokesman for the poor and oppressed. Burke voted against the notorious Stamp Act in 1765 and gave numerous speeches pleading for reconciliation with the American colonies between 1765 and 1776. Burke also took up the cause of the people of India. He believed that British policy towards the native people of India was oppressive and exploitative. Burke worked vigorously for the impeachment of Warren Hastings, a colonial administrator accused of malfeasance during his stay in India. Although Hastings was eventually acquitted, Burke succeeded in raising the social consciousness of the British people regarding the government's colonial policy.

When the French Revolution exploded in 1789, many assumed Burke would take up his pen in defense of the Revolutionaries. This was not to be. Burke saw in the French Revolution a radical uprising devoid of rational thought. Burke essentially predicted the radical phase of the revolution, by anticipating the actions of The Committee of Public Safety and men like Robespierre. Many who had previously respected Burke, men like Thomas Paine, could not forgive Burke for betraying the cause of liberalism. In Burke's view the French Revolution was in itself a betrayal of the cause of liberalism.

(Edmund Burke, a prominent member of the English Parliament, was probably the most noted critic of the French Revolution. In 1790, he wrote Reflections on the Revolution in France, *a resounding denunciation of the French Revolution.)*

Burke's Reflections on the French Revolution (1790)

To make a government requires no great prudence. Settle the seat of power; teach obedience: and the work is done. To give Freedom is still more easy. It is not necessary to guide; it only requires to let go the rein. But to form a *free government;* that is, to temper together these opposite elements of liberty and restraint in one consistent work, requires much thought, deep reflection, a sagacious, powerful and combining mind. This I do not find in those who take the lead in the National Assembly. Perhaps they are not so miserably deficient as they appear. I rather believe it. It would put them below the common level of human understanding. But when the leaders choose to make themselves bidders at an auction of popularity, their talents, in the construction of the state, will be of no service. They will become flatterers instead of legislators; the instruments, not the guides, of the people. If any of them should happen to propose a scheme of liberty, soberly limited, and defined with proper qualifications, he will be immediately outbid by his competitors, who will produce something more splendidly popular. Suspicions will be raised of his fidelity to his cause. Moderation will be stigmatized as the virtue of cowards; and compromise as the prudence of traitors; until, in hopes of preserving the credit which may enable him to temper, and moderate, on some occasions, the popular leader is obliged to become active in propagating doctrines, and establishing powers, that will afterwards defeat any sober purpose at which he ultimately might have aimed.

...The improvements of the National Assembly are superficial, their errors fundamental.

(Edmund Burke, *Reflections on the Revolution in France, in The Works of the Right Honourable Edmund Burke,* 1790)

THOMAS PAINE

(1737-1809)

"Civil Rights are those which appertain to man in right of his being a member of society."

English by birth, Thomas Paine left his native land in 1772 and found his new home in the American Colonies, where he became one of the most eloquent voices for political and individual liberty. Following his authorship of *Common Sense* (1776), in which he advocated America's defiance of England, he produced a series of pamphlets throughout the Revolutionary War. These sixteen essays, known collectively as *The American Crisis*, provided intellectual and emotional energy during some of the most difficult days of the struggle. After the war Paine returned to England and while there wrote *The Rights of Man*, his defense of the French Revolution and a response to its English critics. His attacks on the conservatism of English traditions and institutions led to his prosecution by British authorities, and he fled to France in 1792. Although he had been an eloquent defender of the French Revolution, his participation in the affairs of that country led to his imprisonment for almost a year. During that time he worked on *The Age of Reason*, his famous rationalist assault on the *Bible*. His idealist, radical views turned many against him, not only in England and France, but also in the United States. A 1796 attack in his "Letter to Washington" added to American resentment toward Paine. On his return to the United States in 1802, he was scorned and ignored. He lived in poverty in his final years and died in 1809, leaving behind a legacy of keen thought and powerful prose.

(Edmund Burke's criticism of the French Revolution brought forth numerous replies. One of the most important replies to Burke came from Thomas Paine. Paine wrote The Rights of Man *in an effort to justify the ideals which had brought about the French Revolution.)*

PAINE'S THE RIGHTS OF MAN (1790 AND 1792)

I-Natural and Civil Rights

Among the incivilities by which nations or individuals provoke or irritate each other, Mr. Burke's pamphlet on the French Revolution is an extraordinary instance. There is scarcely an epithet of abuse to be found in the English language with which he has not loaded the French nation and the National Assembly. Considered as an attempt at political argument, his work is a pathless wilderness of rhapsodies, in which he asserts whatever he pleases, without offering evidence or reasons for so doing.

With his usual outrage, he abuses the Declaration of the Rights of Man published by the National Assembly as the basis of the French Constitution. But does he mean to deny that man has any rights? If he does, then he must mean that there are no such things as rights anywhere; for who is there in the world but man? But if Mr. Burke means to admit that man has rights, the question then will be: What are those rights, and how came man by them originally?

The error of those who reason by precedents drawn from antiquity respecting the rights of man is that they do not go far enough into antiquity; they stop in some of the intermediate stages and produce what was then done as a rule for the present day.

Mr. Burke, for example, would have the English nation submit themselves to their monarchs forever, because an English parliament did make such a submission to William and Mary, not only on behalf of the people then living, but on behalf of their heirs and posterities–as if any parliament had the right of binding and controlling posterity, or of commanding forever how the world should be governed.

If antiquity is to be authority, a thousand such authorities may be produced successively contradicting each other; but if we proceed on, we shall at last come out right; we shall come to the time when man came from the hand of his Maker. What was he then? Man! Man was his high and only title, and a higher cannot be given him.

All histories of creation agree in establishing one point, the unity of man, by which I mean that men are all of one degree, and that all men are born equal, and with equal natural rights. Those natural rights are the foundation of all their civil rights.

A few words will explain this. Natural rights are those which appertain to man in right of his existence. Of this kind are the rights of the mind, and also those rights of acting as an individual for his own happiness which are not injurious to the natural rights of others. Civil rights are those which appertain to man in right of his being a member of society. Every civil right has for its foundation some natural right pre-existing in the individual, but to the enjoyment of which his individual power is not, in all cases, competent. Of this kind are all those which relate to security and protection.

It follows, then, that the power produced from the aggregate of natural rights, imperfect in power in the individual, and in which the power to execute is as perfect as the right itself.

Let us now apply these principles to governments. These may all be comprehended under three heads. First, superstition; secondly, power; thirdly, the common interests of society and the common rights of man.

When a set of artful men pretended to hold intercourse with the Deity, as familiarly as they now march up the back stairs in European courts, the world was completely under the government of superstition. This sort of government lasted as long as this sort of superstition lasted.

After these, a race of conquerors arose whose government, like that of William the Conqueror, was founded in power. Governments thus established last as long as the power to support them lasts; but, that they might avail themselves of every engine in their favour, they united fraud to force, and set up an idol which they called "Divine Right" and which twisted itself afterwards into an idol of another shape called "Church and State." The key of St. Peter and the key of the treasury became quartered on one another, and the wondering cheated multitude worshipped the invention.

We have not to review the governments which arise out of society. If we trace government to its origin, we discover that governments must have arisen either out of the people or over the people. In those which have arisen out of the people, the individuals themselves, each in his own personal and sovereign right, have entered into a compact with each other to produce a government; and this is the only mode in which governments have a right to arise.

This compact is the constitution, and a constitution is not a thing in name only, but in fact. Whenever it cannot be produced in a visible form, there is none. A constitution is a thing antecedent to government, and a government is only its creature. The constitution of a country is not the act of its government, but of the people constituting its government.

Can, then, Mr. Burke produce the English constitution? He cannot, for no such thing exists, nor ever did exist. The English government is one of those which arose out of a conquest, and not out of society, and consequently it arose over the people; and though it has been much modified since the time of William the Conqueror, the country has never yet regenerated itself, and is therefore without a constitution.

II-France and England Compared

I now proceed to draw some comparisons between the French constitution and the governmental usages in England.

The French constitution says that every man who pays a tax of sixty sous per annum (2s. 6d. English) is an elector. What will Mr. Burke place against this? Can anything be more limited, and at the same time more capricious, than the qualifications of elections are in England?

The French constitution says that the National Assembly shall be elected every two years. What will Mr. Burke place against this? Why, that the nation has no right at all in the case, and that the government is perfectly arbitrary with respect to this point.

The French constitution says that the right of war and peace is in the nation. Where else should it reside but in those who are to pay the expense? In England this right is said to reside in a metaphor shown at the Tower for sixpence or a shilling a head.

It may with reason be said that in the manner the English nation is represented it signifies not where the right resides, whether in the crown or in the parliament. War is the common harvest of all those who participate in the division and expenditure of public money in all countries. In reviewing the history of the English government, an impartial bystander would declare that taxes were not raised to carry on wars, but that wars were raised to carry on taxes.

The French constitution says, "There shall be no titles"; and, of consequence, "nobility" is done away, and the peer is exalted unto man.

Titles are but nicknames, and every nickname is a title. The thing is perfectly harmless in itself, but it marks a sort of foppery in the human character which degrades it. If no mischief had annexed itself to the folly of titles, they would not have been worth a serious and formal destruction. Let us examine the grounds upon which the French constitution has resolved against having a house of peers.

Because, in the first place, aristocracy is kept up by family tyranny and injustice, due to the unnatural and iniquitous law of primogeniture.

Secondly, because the idea of hereditary legislators is as inconsistent as that of hereditary judges or hereditary juries; and as absurd as an hereditary mathematician, or an hereditary wise man; and as ridiculous as an hereditary poet-laureate.

Thirdly, because a body of men, holding themselves accountable to nobody, ought not to be trusted by anybody.

Fourthly, because it is continuing the uncivilized principle of government founded on conquest, and the base idea of man having property in man and governing him by personal right.

The French constitution hath abolished or renounced toleration and intolerance also, and hath established universal right of conscience. Toleration is not the opposite of intolerance, but is the counterfeit of it. Both are despotisms. The one assumes to itself the right of withholding liberty of conscience, and the other of granting it., Who are thou, vain dust and ashes! by whatever name thou art called, whether a king, a bishop, a church, a state, or a parliament, or anything else, that obtrudest thine insignificance between the soul of man and its maker? Mind thine own concerns. If he believes not as thou believest, it is a proof that thou believest not as he believes and there is no earthly power can determine between you.

The opinions of men with respect to government are changing fast in all countries. The revolutions of America and France have thrown a beam of light over the world, which reaches into men. Ignorance is of a peculiar nature; once dispelled, it is impossible to re-establish it. It is not originally a thing of itself, but is only the absence of knowledge; and though man may be kept ignorant, he cannot be made ignorant.

When we survey the wretched condition of man under the monarchical and hereditary systems of government, dragged from his home by one power, or driven by another, and impoverished by taxes more than by enemies, it becomes evident that these systems are bad and that a general revolution in the principle and construction of governments is necessary.

And it is not difficult to perceive, from the enlightened state of mankind, that hereditary governments are verging to their decline, and that revolutions on the broad basis of national sovereignty and government by representation are making their way in Europe; it would be wisdom to anticipate their approach and produce revolutions by reason and accommodation rather than commit them to the issue of convulsions.

III-The Old and New Systems

The danger to which the success of revolutions is most exposed is in attempting them before the principles on which they proceed, and the advantages to result from them, are sufficiently understood. Almost everything appertaining to the circumstances of a nation has been absorbed and confounded under the general and mysterious word "government." It may, therefore, be of use in this day of revolutions to discriminate between those things which are the effect of government and those which are not.

A great part of that order which reigns among mankind is not the effect of government. It has its origin in the principles of society and the natural constitution of man. The mutual dependence and reciprocal interest which man has upon man, and all parts of civilized community upon each other, create that chain of connexion which holds it together.

The more perfect civilization is, the less occasion has it for government, because the more does it regulate its own affairs and govern itself. All the great laws of society are laws of nature. They are followed and obeyed because it is the interest of the parties to do so, and not on account of any formal laws their government may impose. But how often is the natural propensity to society disturbed or destroyed by the operations of government!

It is impossible that such governments as have hitherto existed in the world would have commenced by any other means than a total violation of every principle, sacred and moral. The obscurity in which the origin of all the present old governments is buried implies the iniquity and disgrace with which they began.

Government on the old system is an assumption of power for the aggrandisement of itself; on the new, a delegation of power for the common benefit of society. The one now called the old is hereditary, either in whole or in part, and the new is entirely representative. It rejects all hereditary government: first as being an imposition on mankind; secondly, as inadequate to the purposes for which government is necessary.

All hereditary government is in its nature tyranny. To inherit a government is to inherit the people, as if they were flocks and herds. Kings succeed each other, not as rationals, but as animals. It signifies not what their mental or moral characters are. Monarchial government appears under all the various character of childhood, decrepitude, dotage; a thing at nurse, in leading-strings, or on crutches. In short, we cannot conceive a more ridiculous figure of government than hereditary succession.

The representative system takes society and civilization for its basis; nature, reason and experience for its guide. The original simple democracy was society governing itself without the aid of secondary means. By ingrafting representation upon democracy we arrive at a system of government capable of embracing and confederating all the various interests and every extent of territory and population; and with advantages as much superior to hereditary government as the republic of letters is to hereditary literature.

Considering government in the only light in which it should be considered, that of a National Association, it ought to be so constructed as not to be disordered by any accident happening among the parts, and, therefore, no extraordinary power should be lodged in the hands of any individual. Monarchy would not have continued so many ages in the world had it not been for the abuses it protects. It is the master-fraud, which shelters all others. By admitting a participation of the spoil, it makes itself friends; and when it ceases to do this it will cease to be the idol of courtiers.

One of the greatest improvements that have been made for the perpetual security and progress of constitutional liberty is the provisions which the new constitutions make for occasionally revising, altering and amending them. The best constitutions that could now be devised may be far short of that excellence which a few years may afford. There is a morning of reason rising upon man on the subject of governments that has not appeared before.

IV-The Reform of England

As it is necessary to include England in the prospect of general reformation, it is proper to inquire into the defects of its government. It is only by each nation reforming its own that the whole can be improved and the full benefit of reformation enjoyed.

When in countries that are called civilized we see age going to the workhouse and youth to the gallows something must be wrong in the system of government. Why is it that scarcely any are executed but the poor? The fact is a proof, among other things, of a wretchedness in their condition. Bred up without morals, and cast upon the world without a prospect, they are the exposed sacrifice of voice and legal barbarity.

The first defect of English government I shall mention is the evil of those Gothic institutions, the corporation towns. As one of the houses of the English parliament is, in a great measure, made up of elections from these corporations, its vices are but a continuation of the vices of its origin.

I proceed in the next place to the aristocracy. The house of peers is simply a combination of persons in one common interest. No better reason can be given why a house of legislation should be composed entirely of men whose occupation consists in letting landed property than why it should be composed of brewers, of bakers, or any other separate class of men. What right has the landed interest to a distinct representation from the general interest of the nation?

I proceed to what is called the crown. It signifies a nominal office of a million sterling a year, the business of which consists in receive the money. Whether the person be wise or foolish, sane or insane, a native or a foreigner, matters not.

I shall now turn to the matter of lessening the burden of taxes. The amount of taxation now levied may be taken in round numbers at £17,000,000, nine millions of which are appropriated to the payment of interest on the national debt, and eight to the current annual expenses.

All circumstances taken together, arising from the French Revolution, from the approaching harmony of the two nations, the abolition of court intrigue on both sides, and the progress of knowledge in the science of governing, the annual expenditure might be put back to one million and a half for navy, army and expenses of government.

Taking one million and a half as a sufficient peace establishment for all the honest purposes of government, there will remain a surplus of upwards of six millions out of the present current expenses. How is this surplus to be disposed of?

The first step would be to abolish the poor rates entirely, and in lieu thereof to make a remission of taxes to the poor of double the amount of the present poor rates—viz., four millions annually out of the surplus taxes. This money could be distributed so as to provide £4 annually per head for the support of children of poor families, and to provide also for the cost of education of over a million children; to give annuities of £10 each for the aged poor over sixty, and of £6 each for the poor over fifty; to give donations of £1 each on occasions of births in poor families and marriages of the poor; to make allowances for funeral expenses of persons travelling for work and dying at the distance from their friends; and to furnish employment for the casual poor of the metropolis where modes of relief are necessary that are not required in the country. Never did so great an opportunity offer itself to England, and to all Europe, as is produced by the two revolutions of America and France. By the former freedom as a national champion in the western world, and by the latter in Europe. When another nation shall join France, despotism and bad government will scarcely dare to appear. The present age will hereafter merit to be called the Age of Reason, and the present generation will appear to the future as the Adam of a new world.

MARY WOLLSTONECRAFT

(1759-1797)

"Women, I allow, may have different duties to fulfill; but they are human duties, and the principles that should regulate the discharge of them, I sturdily maintain, must be the same."

In her *Vindication of the Rights of Women*, Mary Wollstonecraft produced one of the earliest treatises in support of feminism. Born in England in 1759, she lived an unorthodox life, surviving a brutal father and demonstrating through her experiences the intellectual independence and personal freedom that she championed in her writing. Fascinated, as were many in England, by the French Revolution, she spent several years in Paris during the Reign of Terror. While in France, she had an affair with an American, Gilbert Imlay, which resulted in her first child, Fanny, and the eventual separation from her lover. She married William Godwin, an English writer and political philosopher, in 1797. In the same year she died, only days after the birth of another daughter, Mary, who was to become the wife of the Romantic poet Percy Bysshe Shelley and the author of Frankenstein. Other works by Mary Wollstonecraft Godwin include *Thoughts on the Education of Daughters* (1787) and *Historical and Moral Views of the French Revolution* (1794).

(In 1792, Mary Wollstonecraft wrote a treatise in support of the rights of women. Her tract, A Vindication of the Rights of Women, *is still considered an important document in the women's rights movement.)*

Wollstonecraft's A Vindication of the Rights of Women (1792)

It is time to effect a revolution in female mannersótime to restore to them their lost dignity–and make them, as a part of the human species, labour by reforming themselves to reform the world. It is time to separate unchangeable morals from local manners....

I wish to sum up what I have said in a few words, for I here threw down my gauntlet, and deny the existence of sexual virtues, not excepting modesty. For man and woman, truth, if I understand the meaning of the word, must be the same; yet the fanciful female character, so prettily drawn by poets and novelists, demanding the sacrifice of truth and sincerity, virtue becomes a relative idea, having no other foundation than utility, and of that utility men pretend arbitrarily to judge, shaping it to their own convenience.

Women, I allow, may have different duties to fulfil; but they are *human* duties, and the principles that should regulate the discharge of them, I sturdily maintain, must be the same.

To become respectable, the exercise of their understanding is necessary, there is no other foundation for independence of character; I mean explicitly to say that they must only bow to the authority of reason, instead of being the *modest* slaves of opinion.

In the superior ranks of life how seldom do we meet with a man of superior abilities, or even common acquirements? The reason appears to me clear, the state they are born in was an unnatural one. The human character has ever been formed by the employments the individual, or class, pursues; and if the faculties are not sharpened by necessity, they must remain obtuse. The argument may fairly be extended to women; for, seldom occupied by serious business, the pursuit of pleasure gives that insignificancy to their character which renders the society of the great so insipid. The same want of firmness, produced by a similar cause, forces them both to fly from themselves to noisy pleasures, and artificial passions, till vanity takes place of every social affection, and the characteristics of humanity can scarcely be discerned. Such are the blessings of civil governments, as they are at present organized, that wealth and female softness equally tend to debase mankind, and are produced by the same cause; but allowing women to be rational creatures, they should be incited to acquire virtues which they may call their own, for how can a rational being be ennobled by any thing that is not obtained by its own exertions?

(From Mary Wollstonecraft's *A Vindications of the Rights of Women*, 1792)

(On December 15, 1799, the newly formed consulate officially declared the end of the French Revolution. The people were offered a constitution, which was to embody the ideas of the Revolution.)

The Consuls Declare the Revolution Over

Frenchmen!

A Constitution is presented to you.

It terminates the uncertainties which the provisional government introduced into external relations, into the internal and military situation of the Republic.

It places in the institutions which it establishes first magistrates whose devotion has appeared necessary for its success.

The Constitution is founded on the true principles of representative government, on the sacred rights of property, equality, and liberty.

The powers which it institutes will be strong and stable, as they must be in order to guarantee the rights of citizens and the interests of the State.

Citizens, the Revolution is established upon the principles which began it: It is ended.

(From the Constitution of 1799)

PART FIVE

THOMAS ROBERT MALTHUS

(1766-1834)

"Since population is capable of doubling itself at least once every twenty-five years, and since the supply of food can increase in only arithmetical ratio, it follows that increase of population must always be checked by lack of food."

Thomas Robert Malthus was born near Guildford, Surrey, England, in 1766. As an adult he served as an Anglican minister for a short period and then taught economics and history at the East India University at Haileybury, a post he held until his death in 1834. Malthus is most widely known for his treatise on population growth, *An Essay on the Principle of Population*, which he published in 1798. The basic thesis of this essay states that population always has a tendency to outstrip food supply. Additionally, when food supplies are in surplus, the tendency is for population to catch up and eventually exhaust all surpluses. The implication is that most people (the masses) are doomed to lives of hunger and poverty. Malthus's pessimism caused a great stir in the early nineteenth century. Although some used Malthus's essay on population to ridicule efforts to help the poor, Malthus himself called for birth control as a means of halting the population crisis.

Malthus had a profound influence on his own time and influenced such thinkers as Karl Marx, Charles Darwin, Alfred Wallace, David Ricardo, and John Stuart Mill. *An Essay on The Principle of Population* is a powerful line of thinking that demands a response. In many ways modern man is still asking, was Malthus right?

(First published anonymously in 1798, Malthus's Essay on Population is one of the most thought provoking treatises in Western history. Malthus raises the bleak prospect of an over populated world. Aspects of which are still being debated as we enter the twenty-first century.)

ON THE PRINCIPLE OF POPULATION
Thomas Robert Malthus

I — General Survey of the Checks to Population

Since population is capable of doubling itself at least once in every twenty-five years, and since the supply of food can increase in only arithmetical ratio, it naturally follows that increase of population must always be checked by lack of food. But, except in cases of famine, this check is never operative and the chief checks to increase of population are found to be moral restraint, vice and misery.

In spite of these checks, which are always more or less in operation, there is a constant tendency for the population to increase beyond the means of subsistence. Such increase is followed by lowered wages, dearer food and thus a lowered marriage-rate and birth-rate; and the lowered wages, in turn, induce more agricultural enterprise, and thus means of subsistence become more abundant again.

More abundant and cheaper food in turn, promotes marriage and increases the population, until again there is a shortage of food; and this oscillation, though irregular, will always be found, and there will be always a tendency for the population to oscillate around the food limit.

Even among savages, where the degradation of women, infanticide, vice, famine, war and disease are active instruments of decimation, it will be found that the average population, generally speaking, presses hard against the limits of the average food.

Among modern pastoral nations the principal checks which keep the population down to the level of the means of subsistence are: restraint from inability to obtain a wife, vicious habits with respect to women, epidemics, war, famine and the diseases arising from extreme poverty.

In modern Europe we find similar preventive and positive checks, in varying proportions, to undue increase of population. In England and Scotland the preventive check to population prevails in a considerable degree.

A man of liberal education, with an income only just sufficient to enable him to associate in the rank of gentlemen, must feel absolutely certain that if he marry and have a family he shall be obliged to give up all his former connexions. The woman whom a man of education would naturally choose is one brought up in similar refined surroundings. Can a man easily consent to place the object of his affections on a lower social plane? Two or three steps of descent in society, particularly at this round of the ladder, where education ends and ignorance begins, will not be considered by the generality of people as a chimerical, but a real evil. If society be desirable, it surely must be free, equal and reciprocal society, where benefits are conferred as well as received, and not such as the dependent finds with his patrons, or the poor with the rich.

Such considerations certainly prevent many of the better classes from early marriage. Others, possessed of weaker judgement or stronger passion, disregard these considerations; and it would be hard indeed if the gratification of virtuous love did not sometimes more than counterbalance its attendant evils. But those who marry in the face of such considerations too frequently justify the forebodings of the prudent.

The sons of tradesmen and farmers are exhorted not to marry till they have a sufficient sure income to support a family, and often accordingly postpone marriage till they are far advanced in life. The labourer who earns eighteenpence or two shillings a day, as a single man, will hesitate to divide that pittance among four or five, seeing the risks such poverty involves. The servants who live in the families of the rich have yet stronger inducements to forgo matrimony. They live in comparative comfort and luxury, which as married men they could not enjoy.

The prolific power of nature is very far from being called fully into action in Great Britain. And yet, when we contemplate the insufficiency of the price of labour to maintain a large family, and the amount of mortality which arises directly and indirectly from poverty, and add to this the crowds of children prematurely cut off in large towns, we shall be compelled to acknowledge that, if the number born annually were not greatly thinned by this premature mortality, the funds for the maintenance of labour must increase with much greater rapidity than they have ever hitherto done in order to find work and food for the additional numbers that would then grow up to manhood.

Those, therefore, who live single, or marry late, do not by such conduct contribute in any degree to diminish the actual population, but merely to diminish the proportion of premature mortality, which would otherwise be excessive; and consequently, from this point of view, do not seem to deserve any very severe reprobation or punishment.

It has been usual to consider a great proportion of births as the surest sign of a vigorous and flourishing state. But this is erroneous. Only after great mortality, or under very special social conditions, is a large proportion of births a favourable symptom. In the average state of a well-peopled territory there cannot be a worse sign than a large proportion of births, nor a better sign than a small proportion. A small proportion of births is a decided proof of a very small mortality, since the supply always equals the demand for population. In despotic, miserable, or naturally unhealthy countries, the proportion of births to the whole population will generally be found very great.

In Scotland emigration is a potent cause of depopulation; but any thinning out from this cause is quickly neutralized by an increased proportion of births.

In Ireland the details of population fluctuations are little known; but the cheapness of potatoes and the ignorance and depressed, indifferent state of the people, have encouraged marriage to such a degree that the population is pushed much beyond the resources of the country and the consequence, naturally, is that the lower classes of the people are in the most impoverished and miserable state. The checks to the population are, of course, chiefly of the positive kind, and arise from the diseases caused by squalid poverty. To these positive checks have of late years added the vice and misery of civil war and of martial law.

II — Population and the Subsistence Level

That the checks which have been mentioned are the immediate causes of the slow increase of population, and that these checks result principally from an insufficiency of subsistence will be evident from the comparatively rapid increase which has invariably taken place whenever, by some sudden enlargement in the means of subsistence, these checks have been in any considerable degree removed. Plenty of rich land to be had for little or nothing is so powerful a cause of population as generally to overcome all obstacles. The abundance of cheap and profitable land obtained by the colonists of English North America resulted in a rapid increase of population almost without parallel in history. Such an increase does not occur in Britain, and the reason to be assigned is want of food. Want of food is certainly the most efficient of the three immediate checks to population. Population soon increases after war and disease and convulsions of nature, because the food supply is more adequate for the diminished numbers; but where food is deficient no increase of population can occur.

Since the world began, the causes of population and depopulation have been probably as constant as any of the laws of nature with which we are acquainted.

The passion between the sexes has appeared in every age to be so nearly the same that it may always be considered in algebraic language as a given quantity. The great law of necessity, which prevents population from increasing in any country beyond the food which it can either produce or acquire, is a law so obvious and evident to our understandings that we cannot doubt it.

The different modes which nature takes to repress a redundant population do not, indeed, appear to us so certain and regular; but though we cannot always predict the mode, we may with certainty predict the fact. If the proportion of the births to the deaths for a few years indicates an increase of numbers much beyond the proportional increased or acquired food of the country, we may be perfectly certain that, unless an emigration takes place, the deaths will shortly exceed the births, and that the increase which has been observed for a few years cannot be the real average increase of the population of the country.

If there were no other depopulating causes, and if the preventive check did not operate very strongly, every country would, without doubt, be subject to periodical plagues and famines.

The only true criterion of a real and permanent increase in the population of any country is the increase of the means of subsistence, and even this criterion is subject to some slight variations.

Other circumstances being the same, it may be affirmed that countries are populous according to the quantity of human food which they produce or can acquire; and happy according to the liberality with which this food is divided, or the quantity which a day's labour will purchase. This happiness does not depend either upon their being thinly or fully inhabited, upon their poverty or their riches, their youth or age, but on the proportion which the population and the food bear to each other.

In modern Europe the positive checks to population prevail less, and the preventive checks more, than in past times and in the more uncivilized parts of the world, since wars, plagues, acute diseases and famines have become less frequent.

With regard to the preventive checks to population, thought it must be acknowledged that the preventive check of moral restraint does not, at present, largely prevail, yet it is becoming more prevalent, and if we consider only the general term, which implies principally a delay of marriage from prudential considerations, it may be considered as the most potent of the checks which in modern Europe keep down the population to the level of the means of subsistence.

III — Remedies Other Than Moral for Over-Population

All systems of equality which have been proposed are bound to fail, because the motive to the preventive check of moral restraint is destroyed by equality and community of goods. As all would be equal and in similar circumstances, there would be no reason why one person should think himself obliged to practise the duty of restraint more than another. And how could a man be compelled to such restraint? The operation of this natural check of moral restraint depends exclusively upon the existence of the laws of property and succession; and, in a state of equality and community of property could only be replaced by some artificial regulation of a very different stamp, and a much more unnatural character.

No scheme of equality, then, can overcome the population difficulty: emigration is only a palliative and poor-law relief only a nostrum which eventually aggravates the evils of over-population.

The poor laws of England tend to depress the general condition of the poor in two ways. Their first obnoxious tendency is to increase population without increasing the food for its support. A poor man may marry with little or no prospect of being able to support a family without parish assistance. The poor laws may be said, therefore, to create the poor which they maintain, and as the provisions must be distributed to the greater numbers in smaller proportions, the labours of those who are not supported by parish assistance will purchase a smaller quantity of provisions than before, and consequently more of them will require assistance. Secondly, the quantity of provisions consumed in workhouses by the least worthy members of the community diminishes the food of the more worthy members, who are thus driven to obtain relief.

Fortunately for England, a spirit of independence still remains among the peasantry. The poor laws, though calculated to eradicate this spirit, have only partially succeeded. Hard as it may appear in individual instances, dependent poverty ought to be deemed disgraceful. Such a stigma seems necessary to promote the general happiness of mankind. If men be induced to marry from the mere prospect of parish provision, they are not only unjustly tempted to bring unhappiness and dependence upon themselves and their children, but they are tempted unwittingly to injure all in the same class as themselves.

Further, the poor laws discourage frugality and diminish the power and the will of the common people to save, and they live from hand to mouth without thought of the future. A man who might not be deterred from going to the alehouse by the knowledge that his death or sickness might throw his family upon the parish, might fear to waste his earnings if the only provision for it were casual charity.

The mass of unhappiness among common people must be diminished when one of the strongest checks to idleness and dissipation is thus removed; and when institutions which render dependent poverty so lessen the disgrace which should be attached to it. I feel persuaded that if the poor laws had never existed in this country, though there might have been a few more instances of very severe distress, the aggregate mass of happiness among the common people would have been much greater than it is at present. In view of all these facts I do not propose a law to prevent the poor from marrying, but I propose a very gradual abolition of the poor laws.

By means of an extending commerce a country may be able to purchase an increasing quantity of food and to support an increasing population; but extension of commerce cannot continue indefinitely; it must be checked by competition and other economic interference; and as soon as funds for the maintenance of labour become stationary, or begin to decline, there will be no means of obtaining food for an increasing population.

It is the union of the agricultural and commercial systems, and not either of them taken separately, that is calculated to produce the greatest national prosperity. A country with an extensive and rich territory, the cultivation of which is stimulated by improvements in agriculture, manufactures and foreign commerce, has such various and abundant resources that it is extremely difficult to say when they will reach their limits. There are, however, limits to the capital population of a country—limits which they must ultimately reach and cannot pass.

To secure a more abundant and, at the same time, a steadier supply of grain, a system of corn laws has been recommended, the object of which is to discourage, by duties or prohibitions, the importation of foreign corn and to encourage by bounties the exportation of corn of home growth.

Laws which prohibit the importation of foreign grain, though by no means unobjectionable, are not open to the same objections as bounties and must be allowed to be adequate to the object they have in view, the maintenance of an independent supply. Moreover, it is obviously possible, by restrictions upon the importation of foreign corn, to maintain a balance between the agricultural and commercial classes.

The question is not a question of the efficiency or inefficiency of the measure proposed, but of its policy or impolicy. In certain cases there can be no doubt of the impolicy of attempting to maintain an unnatural balance between the agricultural and commercial classes; but in other cases the impolicy is by no means so clear. Restrictions upon the importation of foreign corn in a country which has great landed resources tend not only to spread every commercial and manufacturing advantage possessed, whether permanent or temporary, on the soil, but tend also to prevent those great oscillations in the progress of agriculture and commerce which are seldom unattended with evil.

IV — Moral Restraint and Discriminate Charity

As it appears that in the actual state of every society which has come within our view the natural progress of population has been constantly and powerfully checked, and as it seems evident that no improved form of government, no plans of emigration, no direction of natural industry can prevent the continued action of a great check to population in some form or other, it follows that we must submit to it as an inevitable law of nature, and the only inquiry that remains is how it may take place with the least possible prejudice to the virtue and happiness of human society.

All the immediate checks to population which have been observed to prevail in the same and different countries seem to be resolved into moral restraint, vice and misery; and if our choice be confined to those three, we cannot long hesitate in our decision. It seems certain that moral restraint is the only virtuous and satisfactory mode of escape from the evils of over-population. Without such moral restraint, and if it were the custom to marry at the age of puberty, no virtue, however great, could rescue society from a most wretched and desperate state of want, with its innumerable concomitant diseases and famines.

Prudential restraint, if it were generally adopted, would soon raise the price of labour by narrowing its supply, and those practising it would save money and acquire habits of sobriety, industry and economy such as should ensure happy married life. Further postponement of marriage would give both sexes a better opportunity to choose life-partners wisely and well; and the passion, instead of being extinguished by the experience engendered by early sensuality, would burn the more brightly because repressed for a time and attained as the prize of industry and virtue and as the reward of a genuine attachment.

Moral restraint in this matter is a Christian duty. There are, perhaps, few actions that tend so directly to diminish the general happiness as to marry without being in possession of the means of supporting children. He who commits this act clearly offends against the will of God, for he violates his duty to his neighbours and also to himself, and listens to the voice of passion rather than fulfils the higher obligations of his duty. If he cannot support his children they must starve; and if he marry in the face of a fair probability that he shall not be able to support his children, he is guilty of all the evils which he thus brings upon himself, his wife and his offspring.

When the wages of labour are barely sufficient to support two children, a man marries and has five or six, and finds himself in distress. He blames the low price of labour. He blames the parish and the rich and social institutions but he never blames himself. He may wish he had never married; but it never enters into his head that he has done anything wrong. Indeed, the converse is the case, for he has always been told that to raise up children for his king and country is a very meritorious and patriotic act.

The common people must be taught that they themselves in such a case are to blame and that no one has power to help them if they act thus contrary to the will of God. Those who wish to help the poor must try to raise the relative proportion between the price of labour and the price of provisions, instead of encouraging the poor to marry and over-stock the labour market. A market overstocked with labour and an ample remuneration to each labourer are objects perfectly incompatible.

It is not enough, however, to abolish all the positive institutions which encourage population, but we must endeavour at the same time to correct the prevailing opinions which have the same effect. The public must be made to understand that they have no *right* to assistance and that it is the duty of man not only to propagate his species but to propagate virtue and happiness.

Our private charity must also be discriminate. If we insist that a man shall eat even if he do not work, and that his family shall be supported even if he marry without prospect of supporting a family, we merely encourage worthless poverty. We must not put a premium on idleness and reckless marriages, and we must on no account do anything which tends to remove that inequality of circumstances which ought always to exist between the single man and the man with a family.

KARL MARX
(1818-1883)

"A specter is haunting Europe-the specter of Communism."

Karl Marx was born in the German city of Trier in 1818. A minor government clerk of Jewish descent, Marx's father converted to the Christian faith in order to enhance his career. Marx himself never seems to have acknowledged his Jewish heritage. Marx studied philosophy at the universities of Bonn, Berlin, and Jena. He obtained a doctorate in philosophy, but never gravitated towards the teaching profession. Marx began his work life as a newspaper editor. In 1843 Marx moved to Paris and began a working relationship with Frederick Engels. Engels and Marx were both at work during this period on the analysis of revolutions. Both Marx and Engels were focused on the plight of workers and the need for a Communist form of government.

In 1845 Marx helped to organize a network of Communist Correspondence Committees, that eventually became known as the Communist League, which commissioned Marx and Engels to outline a statement of principles in 1847. This outline resulted in *The Communist Manifesto*, the *Manifesto* was published in 1848, a year in which several revolutionary uprisings took place throughout Europe. The *Manifesto* calls for an immediate uprising of the proletariat by means of a violent revolution. The *Manifesto* soon became the bible for the Communist movement in Europe.

After the publication of the *Manifesto*, Marx found himself even more of an outcast in continental Europe. In 1849 Marx moved his family to London where he spent most of his remaining life. In London Marx committed himself to the writing of his detailed critique of capitalism, *Das Kapital*. The first volume of *Das Kapital* was published in 1867 with two subsequent volumes published after his death. *Das Kapital* represents Marx's attempt at the historical analysis of capitalism and the means by which communism will emerge. Marx's primary influence was on the twentieth century with the promulgation of his ideas by Vladimir Illich Lenin of Russia

(One of the most important developments of the nineteenth century was the growth of Communism. Karl Marx (1818-1883) and Engels, wrote the Communist Manifesto, *which was published in 1848. It is one of the most significant documents in world history.)*

The Communist Manifesto (1848)

A specter is haunting Europe—the specter of Communism. All the powers of old Europe have entered into a holy alliance to exorcise this specter; Pope and Czar, Metternich and Guizot, French radicals and German police spies.

Where is the party in opposition that has not been decried as Communistic by its opponents in power? Where the opposition that has not hurled back the branding reproach of Communism, against the more advanced opposition parties, as well as against its reactionary adversaries?

Two things result from this fact.

I. Communism is already acknowledged by all European powers to be in itself a power.
II. It is high time that Communists should openly, in the face of the whole world, publish their view, their aims, their tendencies, and meet this nursery tale of the Specter of Communism with a Manifesto of the party itself.

To this end the Communists of various nationalities have assembled in London, and sketched the following manifesto to be published in the English, French, German, Italian, Flemish and Danish languages.

In what relation do the Communists stand to the proletarians as a whole? The Communists do not form a separate party opposed to other working class parties.

Of course, in the beginning this cannot be effected except by means of despotic inroads on the rights of property and on the conditions of bourgeois production; by means of measures, therefore, which appear economically insufficient and untenable, but which, in the course of the movement, outstrip themselves, necessitate further inroads upon the old social order and are unavoidable as a means of entirely revolutionizing the mode of production.

These measures will, of course, be different in different countries.

Nevertheless in the most advanced countries the following will be pretty generally applicable:

1. Abolition of property in land and application of all rents of land to public purposes.
2. A heavy progressive or graduated income tax.
3. Abolition of all rights of inheritance.
4. Confiscation of the property of all emigrants and rebels.
5. Centralization of credit in the hands of the State, by means of a national bank with State capital and an exclusive monopoly.
6. Centralization of the means of communication and transport in the hands of the State.
7. Extension of factories and instruments of production owned by the State; the bringing into cultivation of waste lands, and the improvement of the soil generally in accordance with a common plan.
8. Equal liability of all to labor. Establishment of industrial armies, especially for agriculture.
9. Combination of agriculture with manufacturing industries; gradual abolition of the distinction between town and country, by a more equable distribution of the population over the country.
10. Free education for all children in public schools. Abolition of Children's factory labor in its present form. Combination of education with industrial production, etc., etc.

When, in the course of development, class distinctions have disappeared and all production has been concentrated in the hands of a vast association of the whole nation, the public power will lose its political character. Political power, properly so called, is merely the organized power of one class for oppressing another. If the proletariat during its contest with the bourgeoisie is compelled, by the force of circumstances, to organize itself as a class, if, by means of a revolution, it makes itself the ruling class, and, as such, sweeps away by force the old conditions of production, then it will, along with these conditions, have swept away the conditions for the existence of class antagonisms, and of classes generally, and will thereby have abolished its own supremacy as a class.

In place of the old bourgeois society with its classes and class antagonisms we shall have an association in which the free development of each is the condition for the free development of all.

They have no interests separate and apart from those of the proletariat as a whole.

They do not set up any sectarian principles of their own by which to shape and mould the proletarian movement.

The Communists are distinguished from the other working class parties by this only:

1. In the national struggles of the proletarians of the different countries, they point out and bring to the front the common interests of the entire proletariat, independently of all nationality.
2. In the various stages of development which the struggle of the working class against the bourgeoisie has to pass through, they always and everywhere represent the interests of the movement as a whole.

The Communists, therefore, are on the one hand, practically, the most advanced and resolute section of the working class parties of every country, that section which pushes forward all others; on the other hand, theoretically, they have over the great mass of the proletariat the advantage of clearly understanding the line of march, the conditions, and the ultimate general results of the proletarian movement.

The immediate aim of the Communists is the same as that of all the other proletarian parties: formation of the proletariat into a cell, overthrow of the bourgeois supremacy, conquest of political power by the proletariat.

The theoretical conclusions of the Communists are in no way based on ideas or principles that have been invented, or discovered, by this or that would-be universal reformer.

They merely express, in general terms, actual relations springing from an existing class struggle, from a historical movement going on under our very eyes. The abolition of existing property relations is not at all a distinctive feature of Communism.

All property relations in the past have continually been subject to historical change, consequent upon the change in historical conditions.

The French revolution, for example, abolished feudal property in favor of bourgeois property.

The distinguishing feature of Communism is not the abolition of property generally, but the abolition of bourgeois property. But modern bourgeois private property is the final and most complete expression of the system of producing and appropriating products, that is based on class antagonisms, on the exploitation of the many by the few.

In this sense the theory of the Communists may be summed up in the single sentence: Abolition of private property.

We have seen above that the first step in the revolution by the working class is to raise the proletariat to the position of the ruling class; to win the battle of democracy.

The proletariat will use its political supremacy to wrest, by degrees, all capital from the bourgeoisie; to centralize all instruments of production in the hands of the State, i.e., of the proletariat organized as the ruling class; and to increase the total of productive forces as rapidly as possible.

(From Marx's and Engels's *Communist Manifesto*, 1848)

FRIEDRICH ENGELS

(1820-1895)

"English wage earners live from hand to mouth, and this is the distinguishing mark of their proletarian status."

Friedrich Engels was born in Barmen, Germany, in 1820. His father moved the family to Manchester, England, where he owned a textile mill. Engels worked directly for his father in managing the Manchester factory and thus experienced firsthand the plight of the English working class. Engels, much to his father's displeasure, became actively involved in the effort to promote voting rights for the working class in 1842. This Chartist movement, as it became known, was the catalyst for Engels's interest in the Communist movement. In 1844 Engels met Karl Marx, another Communist proponent, and began a collaboration that would last until Marx's death in 1883. Although only slightly younger than Marx, Engels maintained a reverence for Marx throughout their relationship. In 1848 Marx and Engels jointly produced *The Communist Manifesto*.

Engels has often been referred to as the "forgotten partner," given the extreme notoriety of Marx, but his contributions to Communist philosophy were considerable. Besides providing Marx with financial and moral support, Engels produced several important treatises relating to Communist doctrine. In addition, Engels, after the death of Marx, edited the last two volumes of Marx's great opus *Das Kapital*. One of Engels's most important works was his essay *The Condition of the Working Class in England*, in which he discusses the exploitation of the English worker.

(Marx drew heavily from the writings of his colleague Friedrich Engels. Engels was particularly interested in the plight of the working class.)

Engels on the Plight of the Worker

Insecurity is even more demoralising than poverty. English wage-earners live from hand to mouth, and this is the distinguishing mark of their proletarian status. The lower ranks of the German peasantry are largely filled with men who are also poor, and often suffer want, but they are less subject to that sort of distress which is due solely to chance. They do at least enjoy some measure of security. But the proletarian is in quite a different position. He possesses nothing but his two hands and he consumes today what he earned yesterday. His future is at the mercy of chance. He has not the slightest guarantee that his skill will in the future enable him to earn even the bare necessities of life. Every commercial crisis, every whim of his master, can throw him out of work. He is placed in the most revolting and inhuman position imaginable. A slave is at least assured of his daily bread by the self-interest of his master....Slaves and serfs are both guaranteed a basic minimum existence.

The proletarian on the other hand is thrown wholly upon his own resources, and yet at the same time is placed in such a position that he cannot be sure that he can always use those resources to gain a livelihood for himself and his family. Everything that the factory worker can do to try and improve his position vanishes like a drop in the bucket in face of the flood of chance occurrences to which he is exposed and over which he has not the slightest control. He is the passive sufferer from every possible combination of mishaps, and can regard himself as fortunate if he keeps his head above water even for a short time....He may fight for survival in this whirlpool; he may try to maintain his dignity as a human being. This he can do only by fighting the middle classes, who exploit him so ruthlessly and then condemn him to a fate which drives him to live in a way unworthy of a human being.
(Friedrich Engels, *The Condition of the Working Class in England*)

ALEXIS DE TOCQUEVILLE

(1805-1859)

"They had been assured that the inequality of fortunes was as opposed to morality and welfare of society as it was to nature."

Alexis de Tocqueville is best known for his astute observations about the political and social systems of the new republic in North America, presented in a two-volume work, *Democracy in America*, written in the 1830's. His commentary is still considered a classic of political literature. In his native France he was an active and significant voice in politics, especially in the years centering on the Revolution of 1848. In 1849 he served as the French minister of foreign affairs. Although liberal in his social and political sensibilities and a champion of human freedom, he had concerns about the "tyranny of the majority." His views on the advantages and disadvantages of democracy remain useful.

(The French Revolution of the Eighteenth Century was only the first of a series of revolutions in France. Alexis de Tocqueville commented on the French Revolution of 1848.)

De Tocqueville on the June Revolution

I come at last to the insurrection of June....

What distinguished it also, among all the events of this kind which have succeeded one another in France for sixty years, is that it did not aim at changing the form of government, but at altering the order of society.

...It was not, strictly speaking, a political struggle, in the sense which until then we have given to the word, but a combat of class against class, a sort of Servile War. It represented the facts of the Revolution of February in the same manner as the theories of Socialism represented its ideas; or rather it issued naturally from these ideas, as a son does from his mother. We beheld in it nothing more than a blind and rude, but powerful, effort on he part of the workmen to escape from the necessities of their condition, which has been depicted to them as one of unlawful oppression, and to open up by main force a road towards that imaginary comfort with which they had been deluded. It was this mixture of greed and false theory which first gave birth to the insurrection and then made it so formidable. These poor people had been told that the wealth of the rich was in some way the product of a theft practised upon themselves. They had been assured that the inequality of fortunes was as opposed to morality and the welfare of society as it was to nature. Prompted by their needs and their passions, many had believed this obscure and erroneous notion of right, which, mingled with brute force imparted to the latter an energy, a tenacity and a power which it would never have possessed unaided.

It must be observed that this formidable insurrection was not the enterprise of a certain number of conspirators, but the revolt of one whole section of the population against another.

(From de Tocqueville's Journals, 1848)

CHARLES DARWIN

(1809-1882)

"When I view all beings not as special creations, but as the lineal descendents of some few beings which lived long before....they seem to become ennobled."

Charles Darwin was born in Shrewsbury, Shropshire, England, in 1809. He came from a wealthy family and therefore did not have to obtain a profession to earn his way in the world. He graduated from Cambridge University in 1831. While at Cambridge, Darwin became interested in the study of nature and came under the influence of the naturalist John Henslow. In the year he graduated he was afforded the opportunity of working as a naturalist on the survey ship HMS Beagle. This voyage was to help form the foundation of Darwin's theory of evolution.

During the voyage of the Beagle, Darwin was exposed to a vast variety of plant and animal life. He began to question the prevailing theories on natural life and began to develop a thesis that life had evolved over time, rather than having emerged as a result of individual creation. This view, that species were not immutable, was supported by the empirical evidence he encountered on the Galapagos Islands, off the coast of Ecuador. On the Galapagos he noted that each island held animal and plant life that varied slightly from island to island. Darwin concluded that environment plays a role in shaping each species.

The other great influence on Darwin's work was Thomas Malthus's *An Essay on the Principle of Population*. Malthus's central thesis is that life is a struggle between an over-populated planet and its limited resources. Darwin theorized that species evolve in order to best compete for these limited resources. This process he called natural selection. In 1859 Darwin published *On the Origin of Species*, which detailed these findings. Ironically, another Englishman, Alfred Russel Wallace, had reached similar conclusions at almost the exact time. Darwin would later be accused of having stolen several key ideas directly from Wallace's work.

The original printing of *On the Origin of Species* was an immediate success and all initial volumes sold out the first day. Eventually, six editions were needed to quell the demand from the public. Darwin became a controversial figure in that his theories challenged Christian orthodoxy in a very direct way. When he published *The Descent of Man* in 1871, in which he drew direct comparisons of man to animals, the public outcry was enormous. Indeed, society is still debating the nuances of Darwin's theories.

(Charles Darwin's book, The Origin of Species, *1859, argued that a mechanistic view of nature was a superior view of nature; as opposed to nature being subject to the whims of a divine creator.)*

Darwin's View of Nature

Authors of the highest eminence seem to be fully satisfied with the view that each species has been independently created. To my mind it accords better with what we know of the laws impressed on matter by the Creator, that the production and extinction of the past and present inhabitants of the world should have been due to secondary causes, like those determining the birth and death of the individual. When I view all beings not as special creations, but as the lineal descendants of some few beings which lived long before the first bed of the Cambrian [geological] system was deposited, they seem to me to become ennobled....

It is interesting to contemplate a tangled bank, clothed with many plants of many kinds, with birds singing on the bushes, with various insects flitting about, and with worms crawling through the damp earth, and to reflect that these elaborately constructed forms, so different from each other, and dependent upon each other in so complex a manner, have all been produced by laws acting around us. These laws, taken in the largest sense, being Growth with Reproduction; Inheritance which is almost implied by reproduction; Variability from the indirect and direct action of the conditions of life, and from use and disuse: a Ratio of Increase so high as to lead to a Struggle for Life, and as a consequence to natural Selection, entailing Divergence of Character and the Extinction of less-improved forms. Thus, from the war of nature, from famine and death, the most exalted object which we are capable of conceiving, namely the production of the higher animals, directly follows. There is grandeur in this view of life, with its several powers, having been originally breathed by the Creator into a few forms or into one; and that, whilst this planet has gone cycling on according to the fixed law of gravity, from so simple a beginning endless forms most beautiful and most wonderful have been, and are being evolved.

(Charles Darwin, *The Origin of Species and the Descent of Man*, 1859)

OTTO VON BISMARCK

(1815-1898)

"Germany shall be united not by talk, but by iron and blood."

Otto von Bismarck was born in the Brandenburg region of Germany in 1815. Bismarck was from the Junker class and remained loyal to his upper class heritage throughout his political career. After attending the universities at Gottingen and Berlin, Bismarck embarked on a political career. He held several minor political posts and was elected to the Prussian parliament in 1847. A keen supporter of William I's program to update the army, he was appointed premier in 1862. As premier Bismarck began a policy of excluding Austria from the politics of the German state, with an eventual goal of uniting Germany under Hohenzollern rule.

Bismarck undertook three wars to help foster his goal of German unification. In 1864 he persuaded Austria to join him in a war against Denmark in order to gain the territories of Schleswig and Holstein. Then in 1866 he went to war with Austria to solidify Prussian influence among the North German states. His final war against France brought about a unified Germany, as this war stirred the deepest wells of German nationalism. The German Empire was formally declared by Bismarck on January 18, 1871, in the Hall of Mirrors of Versailles.

Bismarck became known as the Iron Chancellor in deference to his Machiavellian tactics. He also pushed through a series of social reforms in Germany, which would serve as a model for other Western nations. Germany was among the first nations to develop a social welfare program; including health insurance, an old age pension program, a limited work day, and limits on child labor. Bismarck's most controversial program was aimed at limiting the power of the Catholic Church in Germany. His Kulturkampf, as it came to be known, limited the role of the Catholic Church in education and political affairs. In 1890 Bismarck was dismissed from service by William II. He was made a Duke but never forgave the emperor for his abrupt dismissal.

(William I of Prussia, on July 13, 1870, sent Bismarck a telegram detailing his conversation with a French Ambassador. The Ems Dispatch, *as it was called, was altered to make the French appear to be demanding.)*

The Ems Dispatch (1870)

THE ORIGINAL MESSAGE SENT BY WILLIAM I TO BISMARCK

"M. Benedetti intercepted me on the Promenade in order to demand of me most insistently that I should authorize him to telegraph immediately to Paris that I shall obligate myself for all future time never again to give my approval to the candidacy of the Hohenzollerns should it be renewed. I refused to agree to this, the last time somewhat severely, informing him that one dare not and cannot assume such obligations *ṭ tout jamais* [forever]. Naturally, I informed him that I had received no news as yet, and since he had been informed earlier than I by way of Paris and Madrid, he could easily understand why my government was once again out of the matter."

Since then His Majesty has received a dispatch from the Prince. As His Majesty has informed Count Benedetti that he was expecting news from the Prince, His Majesty himself, in view of the above-mentioned demand and in consonance with the advice of Count Eulenburg and myself, decided not to receive the French envoy again but to inform him through an adjutant that His Majesty had now received from the Prince confirmation of the news which Benedetti had already received from Paris, and that he had nothing further to say to the Ambassador. His Majesty leaves it to the judgement of Your Excellency whether or not to communicate at once the new demand by Benedetti and its rejection to our ambassadors and to the press.

BISMARCK'S EDITED VERSION
RELEASED TO THE PRESS

After the reports of the renunciation by the Hereditary Prince of Hohenzollern had been officially transmitted by the Royal Government of Spain to the Imperial Government of France, the French Ambassador presented to His Majesty the King at Ems the demand to authorize him to telegraph to Paris that His Majesty the King would obligate himself for all future time never again to give his approval to the candidacy of the Hohenzollerns should it be renewed.

His Majesty the King thereupon refused to receive the French envoy again and informed him through an adjutant that His Majesty had nothing further to say to the Ambassador.

(Excerpt from the *Ems Dispatch*, 1870)

GIUSEPPE MAZZINI

(1805-1872)

"Young Italy is Republican....and dedicated to a united Italy."

Mazzini was born in Genoa in 1805. The son of a doctor, he was given a university education and concentrated on the study of law. In 1815 his native Genoa was absorbed into the Kingdom of Piedmont-Sardinia. Mazzini viewed this annexation as a betrayal of the republican principles of Genoa. In 1827 he joined a society known as the Carbonari. The Carbonari were dedicated to fostering a revolution on the Italian peninsula in order to promote a united Italy under republican rule. Tired of the infighting and general ineffectiveness of the Carbonari, Mazzini formed his own revolutionary society which he dubbed "Young Italy." Mazzini was dedicated to the idea of pushing the Austrians out of Italy by harassing them at every turn and creating a series of mini-uprisings throughout the Italian peninsula.

Mazzini was eventually forced into exile to Switzerland and then to England. During the revolutionary uprisings of 1848, he returned to Italy to help proclaim the Republic of Rome. The new Republic of Rome was short-lived and by the end of 1849 Mazzini was on the run once again. When a united Italy was proclaimed in 1861, Mazzini was profoundly disappointed: his dream of a republican government for Italy had given way to the expediency of a constitutional monarchy set up under the auspices of Piedmont-Sardinia.

Mazzini inspired the move towards a united Italy. Giuseppe Garibaldi and other men dedicated to a united Italy were directly influenced by the rhetoric of Mazzini. While Mazzini died in 1872 disappointed in the fate of his beloved Italy, he can still be connected to the birth of a republican Italy in 1946.

(Mazzini was one of the most important figures in the movement for Italian unity. Consider his motives and to whom he is appealing.)

Mazzini Pleads for Italian Unity

Young Italy is a brotherhood of Italians who believe in the law of *Progress* and *Duty*, and are convinced that Italy is destined to become one nation....They join this association in the firm intent of consecrating both thought and action to the great aim of reconstituting Italy as one independent sovereign nation of free men and equals....

Young Italy is Republican and...dedicated to a United Italy.

The means by which Young Italy proposed to reach its aim are: education and insurrection, to be adopted simultaneously....

The priesthood preach ignorance in the name of the God of truth; and abject submission in the name of the God of battles. They storm against the irreligion, incredulity and wickedness of an epoch which, like all great revolutionary epochs, is essentially religious; against those who, strong in virtue and self-sacrifice, seek to elevate the creature from the dust in the name of the Creator, and restore to man the consciousness of his origin and of his mission; and against enterprises having for their aim the destruction of the anarchy produced by tyranny, and the union of humanity in the name of the spirit of love....Humanity will not stop short because unaccompanied by the depositaries of the ancient creed. The religious idea exists in and for humanity....

You are citizens, you have a country, in order that in a given and limited sphere of action the assistance of a certain number of men, already related to you by language, tendencies and customs, may enable you to labor more effectually for the good of all men....
(From Mazzini's Speeches)

(The European Imperialists of the late 19ᵗʰ century sought to justify the expansion of white European influences. Consider the views of H.S. Chamberlain on race.)

The Role of Race, by H.S. Chamberlain

Nothing is so convincing as the consciousness of the possession of Race. The man who belongs to a distinct, pure race, never loses the sense of it. The guardian angel of his lineage is ever at his side, supporting him where he loses his foothold, warning him like the Socratic Daemon where he is in danger of going astray, compelling obedience, and forcing him to undertakings which deeming them impossible, he would never have dared to attempt. Weak and erring like all that is human, a man of this stamp recognises himself, as others recognise him, by the sureness of his character, and by the fact that his actions are marked by a certain simple and peculiar greatness, which finds its explanation in his distinctly typical and super-personal qualities. Race lifts a man above himself; it endows him with extraordinary—I might almost say supernatural—powers, so entirely does it distinguish him from the individual who springs from the chaotic jumble of peoples drawn from all parts of the world: and should this man of pure origin be perchance gifted above his fellows, then the fact of Race strengthens and elevates him on every hand, and he becomes a genius towering over the rest of mankind, not because he has been thrown upon the earth like a flaming meteor by a freak of nature, but because he soars heavenward like some strong and stately tree, nourished by thousands and thousands of roots—no solitary individual, but the living sum of untold souls striving for the same goal.

(From Chamberlain's Essays)

RUDYARD KIPLING

(1865-1936)

"Take up the White Man's Burden—Ye Dare Not Stoop to Less—"

Rudyard Kipling, the son of a British colonial official, was born in Bombay, India, in 1865. At the age of six Kipling was sent to England to begin his formal education. By 1882 he was back in India working as an editor for a British periodical. Much of Kipling's writing reflects his deep interest in the affairs of India. His most important poems, short stories, and novels are centered on his experiences in India. In 1907 Kipling became the first English author to receive the Nobel Prize in literature.

Despite his love for the customs and land of India, Kipling was an ardent imperialist. He believed it was the destiny of England to rule over lesser nations. This belief proceeded from his conviction that English culture could have a civilizing effect on lesser peoples. In 1899 Kipling wrote his poem *The White Man's Burden*. The poem was written in large part to encourage the American venture in the Philippine Islands. He states that imperialism, while a burden on the conquering nation, is a responsibility that must be met.

KIPLING ADVISES THE AMERICANS: THE RESPONSIBILITY FOR EMPIRE

The White Man's Burden (1899)

(The United States and the Philippine Islands)

Take up the White Man's burden—-
　Send forth the best ye breed—-
Go bind your sons to exile
　To serve your captives' needs;
To wait in heavy harness
　On fluttered folk and wild—-
Your new-caught, sullen peoples,
　Half devil and half child.

Take up the White Man's burden—-
　The savage wars of peace—-
Fill full the mouth of Famine
　And bid the sickness cease;
And when your goal is nearest
　The end for others sought,
Watch Sloth and heathen Folly
　Bring all your hope to nought.
Take up the White Man's burden—-
　And reap his old reward:
The blame of those ye better,
　The hate of these ye guard—-
The cry of hosts ye humour
　(An, slowly!) toward the light:—-
"Why brought ye us from bondage,
　Our loved Egyptian night?"

Take up the White Man's burden—-
   In patience to abide,
To veil the threat of terror
   And check the show of pride;
By open speech and simple,
   An hundred times make plain,
To seek another's profit,
   And work another's gain.
Take up the White Man's burden—-
   No tawdry rule of kings,
But toil of serf and sweeper—-
   The tale of common things.
The ports ye shall not enter,
   The roads ye shall not tread,
Go make them with your living,
   And mark them with your dead!

Take up the White Man's burden—-
   Ye dare not stoop to less—-
Nor call too loud on Freedom
   To cloak your weariness;
By all ye cry or whisper,
   By all ye leave or do,
The silent, sullen peoples
   Shall weigh your Gods and you.

Take up the White Man's burden—-
   Have done with childish days—-
The lightly proffered laurel,
   The easy, ungrudged praise.
Comes now, to search your manhood
   Through all the thankless years,
Cold-edged with dear-bought wisdom,
   The judgment of your peers!

(Rudyard Kipling, *The White Man's Burden*, 1899)

EMILE ZOLA

(1840-1902)

Emile Zola was born in Paris in 1840 and died in 1902. He was a scholarship student at the Lycee Saint Louis in Paris, but he left that school at the age of twenty without earning a degree. Zola suffered through uninspiring work as a clerk, followed by unemployment and poverty until he began to establish himself as a writer. By his thirtieth year he had secured a literary reputation and launched an ambitious project of twenty novels portraying the moral and physical pathologies of the fictitious Rougon family. Included in this series were some of Zola's most enduring works, *Nana* (1880) and *Germinal* (1885). Late in his life he became significantly involved in the famous Dreyfus Affair, siding with the French army captain Alfred Dreyfus, who had been accused and convicted of treason by a military court-martial. The case attracted national and international attention, and Zola, who had attacked the government and the Catholic Church for what he considered prejudiced treatment of Dreyfus, who was a Jew, was himself prosecuted for libel. The article that led to his prosecution was a letter entitled "J'accuse!"

I Accuse.....!

Letter to M. Félix Faure, President of the Republic.

Monsieur le Président:
Will you permit me, in my gratitude for the kindly welcome that you once extended to me, to have a care for the glory that belongs to you, and to say to you that your star, so lucky hitherto, is threatened with the most shameful, the most ineffaceable, of stains?...

And to you, *Monsieur le Président*, will I cry this truth, with all the force of an honest man's revolt. Because of your honor I am convinced that you are ignorant of it. And to whom then shall I denounce the malevolent gang of the really guilty, if not to you, the first magistrate of the country?

First, the truth as to the trial and conviction of Dreyfus.

A calamitous man has managed it all, has done it all—Colonel du Paty de Clam, then a simple major. He is the entire Dreyfus case; it will be fully known only when a sincere investigation shall have clearly established his acts and his responsibilities. He appears as the most heady, the most intricate, of minds, haunted with romantic intrigues, delighting in the methods of the newspaper novel, stolen papers, anonymous letters, meetings in deserted spots, mysterious women who peddle overwhelming proofs by night. It is he who conceived the idea of dictating the *bordereau* to Dreyfus; it is he who dreamed of studying it in a room completely lined with mirrors....

But here is Dreyfus before the council of war. The most absolute secrecy is demanded. Had a traitor opened the frontier to the enemy in order to lead the German emperor to Notre Dame, they would not have taken stricter measures of silence and mystery. The nation is awe-struck; there are whisperings of terrible doings, of those monstrous treasons that excite the indignation of History, and naturally the nation bows. There is no punishment severe enough; it will applaud even public degradation; it will wish the guilty man to remain upon his rock of infamy, eaten by remorse. Are they real then,—these unspeakable things, these dangerous things, capable of setting Europe aflame, which they have had to bury carefully behind closed doors? No, there was nothing behind them save the romantic and mad fancies of Major du Paty de Clam. All this was done only to conceal the most ridiculous of newspaper novels. And, to assure one's self of it, one need only study attentively the indictment read before the council of war....

And we come to the Esterhazy case. Three years have passed; many consciences remain profoundly disturbed, are anxiously seeking, and finally become convinced of the innocence of Dreyfus.

I shall not give the history of M. Scheurer-Kestner's doubts, which later became convictions. But, while he was investigating for himself, serious things were happening to the staff. Colonel Sandherr was dead, and Lieutenant-Colonel Picquart had succeeded him as chief of the bureau of information. And it is in this capacity that the latter, in the exercise of his functions, came one day into possession of a letter-telegram addressed to Major Esterhazy by an agent of a foreign power. His plain duty was to open an investigation. It is certain that he never acted except at the command of his superiors. So he submitted his suspicions to his hierarchical superiors, first to General Gonse, then to General de Boisdeffre, then to General Billot, who had succeeded General Mercier as minister of war. The famous Picquart documents, of which we have heard so much, were never anything but the Billot documents,—I mean, the documents collected by a subordinate for his minister, the documents which must be still in existence in the war department. The inquiries lasted from May to September, 1896, and here it must be squarely affirmed that General Gonse was convinced of Esterhazy's guilt, and that General de Boisdeffre and General Billot had no doubt that the famous *bordereau* was in Esterhazy's handwriting. Lieutenant-Colonel Picquart's investigation had ended in the certain establishment of this fact. But the emotion thereat was great, for Esterhazy's conviction inevitably involved a revision of the Dreyfus trial; and this the staff was determined to avoid at any cost....

Colonel Picquart had done his duty as an honest man. He insisted in the presence of his superiors, in the name of justice; he even begged of them; he told them how impolitic were their delays, in view of the terrible storm which was gathering, and which would surely burst as soon as the truth should be known....

Such, then, is the simple truth, *Monsieur le Président*, and it is frightful. It will remain a stain upon your presidency. I suspect that you are powerless in this matter,—that you are the prisoner of the constitution and of your environment. You have none the less a man's duty, upon which you will reflect, and which you will fulfill. Not indeed that I despair, the least in the world, of triumph. I repeat with more vehement certainty; truth is on the march, and nothing can stop it. To-day sees the real beginning of the affair, since not until to-day have the positions been clear: on one hand, the guilty, who do not want the light; on the other, the doers of justice, who will give their lives to get it. When truth is buried in the earth, it accumulates there, and assumes so mighty an explosive power that, on the day when it bursts forth, it hurls everything into the air. We shall see if they have not just made preparations for the most resounding of disasters, yet to come.

But this letter is long, *Monsieur le Président*, and it is time to finish.

I accuse Lieutenant-Colonel du Paty de Clam of having been the diabolical workman of judicial error,—unconsciously, I am willing to believe,—and of having then defended his calamitous work, for three years, by the most guilty machinations.

I accuse General Mercier of having made himself an accomplice, at least through weakness of mind, in one of the greatest iniquities of the century.

I accuse General Billot of having had in his hands certain proofs of the innocence of Dreyfus, and of having stifled them; of having rendered himself guilty of this crime of *lése-humanité* and *lése-justice* for a political purpose, and to save the compromised staff.

I accuse General de Boisdeffre and General Gonse of having made themselves accomplices in the same crime, one undoubtedly through clerical passion, the other perhaps through that *esprit de corps* which makes of the war offices the Holy Ark, unassailable.

I accuse General de Pellieux and Major Ravary of having conducted a rascally inquiry,—I mean by that a monstrously partial inquiry, of which we have, in the report of the latter, an imperishable monument of naive audacity.

I accuse the three experts in handwriting, Belhomme, Varinard, and Couard, of having made lying and fraudulent reports, unless a medical examination should declare them afflicted with diseases of the eye and of the mind.

I accuse the war offices of having carried on in the press, particularly in "L 'Eclair" and in "L 'Echo de Paris," an abominable campaign, to mislead opinion and cover up their faults.

I accuse, finally, the first council of war of having violated the law by condemning an accused person on the strength of a secret document, and I accuse the second council of war of having covered this illegality, in obedience to orders, in committing in its turn the judicial crime of knowingly acquitting a guilty man.

In preferring these charges, I am not unaware that I lay myself liable under Articles 30 and 31 of the press law of July 29, 1881, which punishes defamation. And it is willfully that I expose myself thereto.

As for the people whom I accuse, I do not know them, I have never seen them, I entertain against them no feeling of revenge or hatred. They are to me simple entities, spirits of social ill-doing. And the act that I perform here is nothing but a revolutionary measure to hasten the explosion of truth and justice.

I have but one passion, the passion for the light, in the name of humanity which has suffered so much, and which is entitled to happiness. My fiery protest is simply the cry of my soul. Let them dare, then, to bring me into the assize court, and let the investigation take place in the open day.

I await it.

Accept, *Monsieur le Président*, the assurance of my profound respect.

Emile Zola.

(The Trial of Emile Zola (New York: Ben R. Tucker, 1898), pp. 3, 4, 6, 7-8, 9, 13-14.)

JOHN STUART MILL

(1806-1873)

"It is better to be a human being dissatisfied than a pig satisfied; better to be Socrates dissatisfied than a fool satisfied. And if the fool, or the pig, are of a different opinion, it is because they only know their own side of the question. The other party to the comparison knows both sides."

    Although Jeremy Bentham first voiced in England the political and philosophical principles that came to be known as Utilitarianism, it was John Stuart Mill, encouraged by his father James, who became the foremost spokesman for the radical social view that championed "the greatest good for the greatest number."

    Utilitarian thinkers, as emphasized by Mill in the following excerpt, traced the origin of their moral system to Epicurus, but Mill's formulation of the philosophy departs from the Greek's traditional hedonism on two important points. Mill argues that some pleasures, are superior to others intrinsically, as well as circumstantially. He also observes that the pursuit of pleasure has ennobling consequences, evolving from egoism to altruism.

UTILITARIANISM
JOHN STUART MILL

What Utilitarianism Is

The creed which accepts as the foundation of morals "utility" or the "greatest happiness principle" holds that actions are right in proportion as they tend to promote happiness; wrong as they tend to produce the reverse of happiness. By happiness is intended pleasure and the absence of pain; by unhappiness, pain and the privation of pleasure. To give a clear view of the moral standard set up by the theory, much more requires to be said; in particular, what things it includes in the ideas of pain and pleasure, and to what extent this is left an open question. But these supplementary explanations do not affect the theory of life on which this theory of morality is grounded—namely, that pleasure and freedom from pain are the only things desirable as ends; and that all desirable things (which are as numerous in the utilitarian as in any other scheme) are desirable either for pleasure inherent in themselves or as means to the promotion of pleasure and the prevention of pain.

Now such a theory of life excites in many minds, and among them in some of the most estimable in feeling and purpose, inveterate dislike. To suppose that life has (as they express it) no higher end than pleasure—no better and nobler object of desire and pursuit—they designate as utterly mean and groveling, as a doctrine worthy only of swine, to whom the followers of Epicurus were, at a very early period, contemptuously likened; and modern holders of the doctrine are occasionally made the subject of equally polite comparisons by its German, French, and English assailants.

When thus attacked, the Epicureans have always answered that it is not they, but their accusers, who represent human nature in a degrading light, since the accusation supposes human beings to be capable of no pleasures except those of which swine are capable. If this supposition were true, the charge could not be gainsaid, but would then be no longer an imputation; for if the sources of pleasure were precisely the same to human beings and to swine, the rule of life which is good enough for the one would be good enough for the other. The comparison of the Epicurean life to that of beasts is felt as degrading, precisely because a beast's pleasures do not satisfy a human being's conceptions of happiness. Human beings have faculties more elevated than the animal appetites and, when once made conscious of them, do not regard anything as happiness which does not include their gratification. I do not, indeed, consider the Epicureans to have been by any means faultless in drawing out their scheme of consequences from the utilitarian principle. To do this in any sufficient manner, many Stoic, as well as Christian, elements require to be included. But there is no known Epicurean theory of life which does not assign to the pleasures of the intellect, of the feelings and imagination, and of the moral sentiments a much higher value as pleasures than to those of mere sensation. It must be admitted, however, that utilitarian writers in general have placed the superiority of mental over bodily pleasures chiefly in the greater permanency, safety, uncostliness, etc., of the former—that is, in their circumstantial advantages rather than in their intrinsic nature. And on all these points utilitarians have fully proved their case; but they might have taken the other and, as it may be called, higher ground with entire consistency. It is quite compatible with the principle of utility to recognize the fact that some kinds of pleasure are more desirable and more valuable than others. It would be absurd that, while in estimating all other things quality is considered as well as quantity, the estimation of pleasure should be supposed to depend on quantity alone.

If I am asked what I mean by difference of quality in pleasures, or what makes one pleasure more valuable than another, merely as a pleasure, except its being greater in amount, there is but one possible answer. Of two pleasures, if there be one to which all or almost all who have experience of both give a decided preference, irrespective of any feeling of moral obligation to prefer it, that is the more desirable pleasure. If one of the two is, by those who are competently acquainted with both, placed so far above the other that they prefer it, even though knowing it to be attended with a greater amount of discontent, and would not resign it for any quantity of the other pleasure which their nature is capable of, we are justified in ascribing to the preferred enjoyment a superiority in quality so far outweighing quantity as to render it, in comparison, of small account. Now it is an unquestionable fact that those who are equally acquainted with and equally capable of appreciating and enjoying both do give a most marked preference to the manner of existence which employs their higher faculties. Few human creatures would consent to be changed into any of the lower animals for a promise of the fullest allowance of a beast's pleasures; no intelligent human being would consent to be a fool, no instructed person would be an ignoramus, no person of feeling and conscience would be selfish and base, even though they should be persuaded that the fool, the dunce, or the rascal is better satisfied with his lot than they are with theirs. They would not resign what they possess more than he for the most complete satisfaction of all the desires which they have in common with him. If they ever fancy they would, it is only in cases of unhappiness so extreme that to escape from it they would exchange their lot for almost any other, however undesirable in their own eyes. A being of higher faculties requires more to make him happy, is capable probably of more acute suffering, and certainly accessible to it at more points, than one of an inferior type; but in spite of these liabilities, he can never really wish to sink into what he feels to be a lower grade of existence. We may give what explanation we please of this unwillingness; we may attribute it to pride, a name which is given indiscriminately to some of the most and to some of the least estimable feelings of which mankind are capable; we may refer it to the love of liberty and personal independence, an appeal to which was with the Stoics one of the most effective means for the inculcation of it; to the love of power or to the love of excitement, both of which do really enter into and contribute to it; but its most appropriate appellation is a sense of dignity, which all human beings possess in one form or other, and in some, though by no means in exact, proportion to their higher faculties, and which is so essential a part of the happiness of those in whom it is strong that nothing which conflicts with it could be otherwise than momentarily an object of desire to them. Whoever supposes that this preference takes place at a sacrifice of happiness—that the superior being, in anything like equal circumstances, is not happier than the inferior—confounds the two very different ideas of happiness and content. It is indisputable that the being whose capacities of enjoyment are low has the greatest chance of having them fully satisfied; and a highly endowed being will always feel that any happiness which he can look for, as the world is constituted, is imperfect. But he can learn to bear its imperfections, if they are at all bearable; and they will not make him envy the being who is indeed unconscious of the imperfections, but only because he feels not at all the good which those imperfections qualify. It is better to be a human being dissatisfied than a pig satisfied; better to be Socrates dissatisfied than a fool satisfied. And if the fool, or the pig, are of a different opinion, it is because they only know their own side of the question. The other party to the comparison knows both sides.

It may be objected that many who are capable of the higher pleasures occasionally, under the influence of temptation, postpone them to the lower. But this is quite compatible with a full appreciation of the intrinsic superiority of the higher. Men often, from infirmity of character, make their election for the nearer good, though they know it to be the less valuable; and this no less when the choice is between two bodily pleasures than when it is between bodily and mental. They pursue sensual indulgences to the injury of health, though perfectly aware that health is the greater good. It may be further objected that many who begin with youthful enthusiasm for everything noble, as they advance in years, sink into indolence and selfishness. But I do not believe that those who undergo this very common change voluntarily choose the lower description of pleasures in preference to the higher. I believe that, before they devote themselves exclusively to the one, they have already become incapable of the other. Capacity for the nobler feelings is in most natures a very tender plant, easily killed, not only by hostile influences, but by mere want of sustenance; and in the majority of young persons it speedily dies away if the occupations to which their position in life has devoted them, and the society into which it has thrown them, are not favorable to keeping that higher capacity in exercise. Men lose their high aspirations as they lose their intellectual tastes, because they have not time or opportunity for indulging them; and they addict themselves to inferior pleasures, not because they deliberately prefer them, but because they are either the only ones to which they have access or the only ones which they are any longer capable of enjoying. It may be questioned whether anyone who has remained equally susceptible to both classes of pleasures ever knowingly and calmly preferred the lower, though many, in all ages, have broken down in an ineffectual attempt to combine both.

From this verdict of the only competent judges, I apprehend there can be no appeal. On a question which is the best worth having of two pleasures, or which of two modes of existence is the most grateful to the feelings, apart from its moral attributes and from its consequences, the judgment of those who are qualified by knowledge of both, or, if they differ, that of the majority among them, must be admitted as final. And there needs be the less hesitation to accept this judgment respecting the quality of pleasures, since there is no other tribunal to be referred to even on the question of quantity. What means are there of determining which is the acutest of two pains, or the intensest of two pleasurable sensations, except the general suffrage of those who are familiar with both? Neither pains nor pleasures are homogeneous, and pain is always heterogeneous with pleasure. What is there to decide whether a particular pleasure is worth purchasing at the cost of a particular pain, except the feelings and judgment of the experienced? When, therefore, those feelings and judgment declare the pleasures derived from the higher faculties to be preferable *in kind,* apart from the question of intensity, to those of which the animal nature, disjoined from the higher faculties, is susceptible, they are entitled on this subject to the same regard.

I have dwelt on this point as being a necessary part of a perfectly just conception of utility or happiness considered as the directive rule of human conduct. But it is by no means an indispensable condition to the acceptance of the utilitarian standard; for that standard is not the agent's own greatest happiness, but the greatest amount of happiness altogether; and if it may possibly be doubted whether a noble character is always the happier for its nobleness, there can be no doubt that it makes other people happier, and that the world in general is immensely a gainer by it. Utilitarianism, therefore, could only attain its end by the general cultivation of nobleness of character, even if each individual were only benefited by the nobleness of others, and his own, so far as happiness is concerned, were a sheer deduction from the benefit. But the bare enunciation of such an absurdity as this last renders refutation superfluous.

According to the greatest happiness principle, as above explained, the ultimate end, with reference to and for the sake of which all other things are desirable—whether we are considering our own good or that of other people—is an existence exempt as far as possible from pain, and as rich as possible in enjoyments, both in point of quantity and quality; the test of quality and the rule for measuring it against quantity being the preference felt by those who, in their opportunities of experience, to which must be added their habits of self-consciousness and self-observation, are best furnished with the means of comparison. This, being according to the utilitarian opinion the end of human action, is necessarily also the standard of morality, which may accordingly be defined "the rules and precepts for human conduct," by the observance of which an existence such as has been described might be, to the greatest extent possible, secured to all mankind; and not to them only, but, so far as the nature of things admits, to the whole sentient creation.

Against this doctrine, however, arises another class of objectors who say that happiness, in any form, cannot be the rational purpose of human life and action; because, in the first place, it is unattainable; and they contemptuously ask, What right hast thou to be happy?—a question which Mr. Carlyle clinches by the addition, What right, a short time ago, hadst thou even *to be?* Next they say that men can do *without* happiness; that all noble human beings have felt this, and could not have become noble but by learning the lesson of *Entsagen,* or renunciation: which lesson, thoroughly learned and submitted to, they affirm to be the beginning and necessary condition of all virtue.

The first of these objections would go to the root of the matter were it well founded; for if no happiness is to be had at all by human beings, the attainment of it cannot be the end of morality or of any rational conduct. Though, even in that case, something might still be said for the utilitarian theory, since utility includes not solely the pursuit of happiness, but the prevention or mitigation of unhappiness; and if the former aim be chimerical, there will be all the greater scope and more imperative need for the latter, so long at least as mankind think fit to live and do not take refuge in the simultaneous act of suicide recommended under certain conditions by Novalis. When, however, it is thus positively asserted to be impossible that human life should be happy, the assertion, if not something like a verbal quibble, is at least an exaggeration. If by happiness be meant a continuity of highly pleasurable excitement, it is evident enough that this is impossible. A state of exalted pleasure lasts only moments or in some cases, and with some intermissions, hours or days, and is the occasional brilliant flash of enjoyment, not its permanent and steady flame. Of this the philosophers who have taught that happiness is the end of life were as fully aware as those who taunt them. The happiness which they meant was not a life of rapture, but moments of such, in an existence made up of few and transitory pains, many and various pleasures, with a decided predominance of the active over the passive, and having as the foundation of the whole not to expect more from life than it is capable of bestowing. A life thus composed, to those who have been fortunate enough to obtain it, has always appeared worthy of the name of happiness. And such an existence is even now the lot of many during some considerable portion of their lives. The present wretched education and wretched social arrangements are the only hindrance to its being attainable by almost all.

  The objectors perhaps may doubt whether human beings, if taught to consider happiness as the end of life, would be satisfied with such a moderate share of it. But great numbers of mankind have been satisfied with much less. The main constituents of a satisfied life appear to be two, either of which by itself is often found sufficient for the purpose: tranquility and excitement. With such tranquility, many find that they can be content with very little pleasure; with much excitement, many can reconcile themselves to a considerable quantity of pain. There is assuredly no inherent impossibility of enabling even the mass of mankind to unite both, since the two are so far from being incompatible that they are in natural alliance, the prolongation of either being a preparation for, and exciting a wish for, the other. It is only those in whom indolence amounts to a vice that do not desire excitement after an interval of repose; it is only those in whom the need of excitement is a disease that feel the tranquility which follows excitement dull and insipid, instead of pleasurable in direct proportion to the excitement which preceded it. When people who are tolerably fortunate in their outward lot do not find in life sufficient enjoyment to make it valuable to them, the cause generally is caring for nobody but themselves. To those who have neither public nor private affections, the excitements of life are much curtailed, and in any case dwindle in value as the time approaches when all selfish interests must be terminated by death; while those who leave after them objects of personal affection, and especially those who have also cultivated a fellow-feeling with the collective interests of mankind, retain as lively an interest in life on the eve of death as in the vigor of youth and health. Next to selfishness, the principal cause which makes life unsatisfactory is want of mental cultivation. A cultivated mind—I do not mean that of a philosopher, but any mind to which the fountains of knowledge have been opened, and which has been taught, in any tolerable degree, to exercise its faculties—finds sources of inexhaustible interest in all that surrounds it: in the objects of nature, the achievements of art, the imaginations of poetry, the incidents of history, the ways of mankind, past and present, and their prospects in the future. It is possible, indeed, to become indifferent to all this, and that too without having exhausted a thousandth part of it, but only when one has had from the beginning no moral or human interest in these things and has sought in them only the gratification of curiosity.

Now there is absolutely no reason in the nature of things why an amount of mental culture sufficient to give an intelligent interest in these objects of contemplation should not be the inheritance of everyone born in a civilized country. As little is there an inherent necessity that any human being should be a selfish egotist, devoid of every feeling or care but those which center in his own miserable individuality. Something far superior to this is sufficiently common even now, to give ample earnest of what the human species may be made. Genuine private affections and a sincere interest in the public good are possible, though in unequal degrees, to every rightly brought up human being. In a world in which there is so much to interest, so much to enjoy, and so much also to correct and improve, everyone who has this moderate amount of moral and intellectual requisites is capable of an existence which may be called enviable; and unless such a person, through bad laws or subjection to the will of others, is denied the liberty to use the sources of happiness within his reach, he will not fail to find this enviable existence, if he escape the positive evils of life, the great sources of physical and mental suffering—such as indigence, disease, and the unkindness, worthlessness, or premature loss of objects of affection. The main stress of the problem lies, therefore, in the contest with these calamities from which it is a rare good fortune entirely to escape; which, as things now are, cannot be obviated, and often cannot be in any material degree mitigated. Yet no one whose opinion deserves a moment's consideration can doubt that most of the great positive evils of the world are in themselves removable, and will, if human affairs continue to improve, be in the end reduced within narrow limits. Poverty, in any sense implying suffering, may be completely extinguished by the wisdom of society combined with the good sense and providence of individuals. Even that most intractable of enemies, disease, may be indefinitely reduced in dimensions by good physical and moral education and proper control of noxious influences, while the progress of science holds out a promise for the future of still more direct conquests over this detestable foe. And every advance in that direction relieves us from some, not only of the chances which cut short our own lives, but, what concerns us still more, which deprive us of those in whom our happiness is wrapt up. As for vicissitudes of fortune and other disappointments connected with worldly circumstances, these are principally the effect either of gross imprudence, of ill-regulated desires, or of bad or imperfect social institutions. All the grand sources, in short, of human suffering are in a great degree, many of them almost entirely, conquerable by human care and effort; and though their removal is grievously slow—though a long succession of generations will perish in the breach before the conquest is completed, and this world becomes all that, if will and knowledge were not wanting, it might easily be made—yet every mind sufficiently intelligent and generous to bear a part, however small and inconspicuous, in the endeavor will draw a noble enjoyment from the contest itself, which he would not for any bribe in the form of selfish indulgence consent to be without.

FRIEDRICH NIETZSCHE

(1844-1900)

"'Exploitation' does not belong to a depraved, or imperfect and primitive society: it belongs to the nature of the living being as a primary organic function..."

Friedrich Nietzsche was born in the region of Saxony (now part of Germany) in 1844. His father was a Lutheran minister who died when Nietzsche was only five years old. It was intended that young Friedrich was to study theology, but he eventually decided on a career in philology at universities in Bonn and Leipzig. He excelled as a student and was eventually appointed to a prestigious teaching position in Basel. His poor health eventually forced him from the field of teaching. After his teaching career ended, Nietzsche began to write works which place less emphasis on scholarly attainment and more emphasis on his personal philosophy.

One consistent theme in the works of Nietzsche is his challenge to convention. Nietzsche believed that the standards (morals) of society serve only to inhibit personal growth and place mankind into subservient roles. He views traditional philosophy and religion as particularly harmful to humanity. These institutions ask us to take marching orders and place us in the position of being slaves to their rules. *Beyond Good and Evil* consists of a series of critiques of the Western tradition. In this work he challenges us to consider when and why these "rules of society" came about. He urges the individual to create a truth based on self-reflection and personal understanding.

Virtually no tradition is spared the wrath of Nietzsche's pen. Despite his early lapse into insanity around 1890, Nietzsche's work has intrigued virtually every generation that has come after him. He has been called "the philosopher" for the twentieth century.

BEYOND GOOD AND EVIL
FRIEDRICH NIETZSCHE

Every elevation of the type "man," has hitherto been the work of an aristocratic society and so it will always be—a society believing in a long scale of gradations of rank and differences of worth among human beings, and requiring slavery in some form or other. Without the *pathos of distance,* such as grows out of the incarnated difference of classes, out of the constant outlooking and downlooking of the ruling caste on subordinates and instruments, and out of their equally constant practice of obeying and commanding, of keeping down and keeping at a distance—that other more mysterious pathos could never have arisen, the longing for an ever new widening of distance within the soul itself, the formation of ever higher, rarer, further, more extended, more comprehensive states, in short, just the elevation of the type "man," the continued "self-surmounting of man," to use a moral formula in a supermoral sense. To be sure, one must not resign oneself to any humanitarian illusions about the history of the origin of an aristocratic society (that is to say, of the preliminary condition for the elevation of the type "man"): the truth is hard. Let us acknowledge unprejudicedly how every higher civilisation hitherto has *originated!* Men with a still natural nature, barbarians in every terrible sense of the word, men of prey, still in possession of unbroken strength of will and desire for power, threw themselves upon weaker, more moral, more peaceful races (perhaps trading or cattle-rearing communities), or upon old mellow civilisations in which the final vital force was flickering out in brilliant fireworks of wit and depravity. At the commencement, the noble caste was always the barbarian caste: their superiority did not consist first of all in their physical, but in their psychical power—they were more *complete* men (which at every point also implies the same as "more complete beasts).

Corruption—as the indication that anarchy threatens to break out among the instincts, and that the foundation of the emotion, called "life," is convulsed—is something radically different according to the organisation in which it manifests itself. When, for instance, an aristocracy like that of France at the beginning of the Revolution, flung away its privileges with sublime disgust and sacrificed itself to an excess of its moral sentiments, it was corruption:—it was really only the closing act of the corruption which had existed for centuries, by virtue of which that aristocracy had abdicated step by step its lordly prerogatives and lowered itself to a *function* of royalty (in the end even to its decoration and parade-dress). The essential thing, however, in a good and healthy aristocracy is that it should *not* regard itself as a function either of the kingship or the commonwealth, but as the *significance* and highest justification thereof—that it should therefore accept with a good conscience the sacrifice of a legion of individuals, who, *for its sake,* must be suppressed and reduced to imperfect men, to slaves and instruments. Its fundamental belief must be precisely that society is *not* allowed to exist for its own sake, but only as a foundation and scaffolding, by means of which a select class of beings may be able to elevate themselves to their higher duties, and in general to a higher *existence*: like those sun-seeking climbing plants in Java—they are called *Sipo Matador,*—which encircle an oak so long and so often with their arms, until at last, high above it, but supported by it, they can unfold their tops in the open light, and exhibit their happiness.

To refrain mutually from injury, from violence, from exploitation, and put one's will on a par with that of others: this may result in a certain rough sense in good conduct among individuals when the necessary conditions are given (namely, the actual similarity of the individuals in amount of force and degree of worth, and their co-relation within one organisation). As soon, however, as one wished to take this principle more generally, and if possible even as *the fundamental principle of society,* it would immediately disclose what it really is—namely, a Will to the *denial* of life, a principle of dissolution and decay. Here one must think profoundly to the very basis and resist all sentimental weakness: life itself is *essentially* appropriation, injury, conquest of the strange and weak, suppression, severity, obtrusion of peculiar forms, incorporation, and at the least, putting it mildest, exploitation;—but why should one for ever use precisely these words on which for ages a disparaging purpose has been stamped? Even the organisation within which, as was previously supposed, the individuals treat each other as equal—it takes place in every healthy aristocracy—must itself, if it be a living and not a dying organisation, do all that towards other bodies, which the individuals within it refrain from doing to each other: it will have to be the incarnated Will to Power, it will endeavour to grow, to gain ground, attract to itself and acquire ascendency—not owing to any morality or immorality, but because it *lives,* and because life *is* precisely Will to Power. On no point, however, is the ordinary consciousness of Europeans more unwilling to be corrected than on this matter; people now rave everywhere, even under the guise of science, about coming conditions of society in which "the exploiting character" is to be absent:—that sounds to my ears as if they promised to invent a mode of life which should refrain from all organic functions. "Exploitation" does not belong to a depraved, or imperfect and primitive society: it belongs to the *nature* of the living being as a primary organic function; it is a consequence of the intrinsic Will to Power, which is precisely the Will to Life.—Granting that as a theory this is a novelty—as a reality it is the *fundamental fact* of all history: let us be so far honest towards ourselves!

In a tour through the many finer and coarser moralities which have hitherto prevailed or still prevail on the earth, I found certain traits recurring regularly together, and connected with one another, until finally two primary types revealed themselves to me, and a radical distinction was brought to light. There is *master-morality* and *slave-morality;*—I would at once add, however, that in all higher and mixed civilisations, there are also attempts at the reconciliation of the two moralities; but one finds still oftener the confusion and mutual misunderstanding of them, indeed, sometimes their close juxtaposition—even in the same man, within one soul. The distinctions of moral values have either originated in a ruling caste, pleasantly conscious of being different from the ruled—or among the ruled class, the slaves and dependents of all sorts. In the first case, when it is the rulers who determine the conception "good," it is the exalted, proud disposition which is regarded as the distinguishing feature, and that which determines the order of rank. The noble type of man separates from himself the beings in whom the opposite of this exalted, proud disposition displays itself: he despises them. Let it at once be noted that in this first kind of morality the antithesis "good" and "bad" means practically the same as "noble" and "despicable";—the antithesis "good" and *"evil"* is of different origin. The cowardly, the timid, the insignificant, and those thinking merely of narrow utility are despised; moreover, also, the distrustful, with their constrained glances, the self-abasing, the doglike kind of men who let themselves be abused, the mendicant flatterers, and above all the liars:—it is a fundamental belief of all aristocrats that the common people are untruthful. "We truthful ones"—the nobility in ancient Greece called themselves. It is obvious that everywhere the designations of moral value were at first applied to *men,* and were only derivatively and at a later period applied to *actions;* it is a gross mistake, therefore, when historians of morals start with questions like, "Why have sympathetic actions been praised?" The noble type of man regards *himself* as a determiner of values; he does not require to be approved of; he passes the judgment: "What is injurious to me is injurious in itself"; he knows that it is he himself only who confers honour on things; he is a *creator of values.* He honours whatever he recognises in himself: such morality is self-glorification. In the foreground there is the feeling of plenitude, of power, which seeks to overflow, the happiness of high tension, the consciousness of a wealth which would fain give and bestow:—the noble man also helps the unfortunate, but not—or scarcely—out of pity, but rather from an impulse generated by the super-abundance of power. The noble man honours in himself the powerful one, him also who has power over himself, who knows how to speak and how to keep silence, who takes pleasure in subjecting himself to severity and hardness, and has reverence for all that is severe and hard. "Wotan placed a hard heart in my breast," says an old Scandinavian Saga: it is thus rightly expressed from the soul of a proud Viking. Such a type of man is even proud of *not* being made for sympathy; the hero of the

Saga therefore adds warningly: "He who has not a hard heart when young, will never have one." The noble and brave who think thus are the furthest removed from the morality which sees precisely in sympathy, or in acting for the good of others, or in *désintéressement,* the characteristic of the moral; faith in oneself, pride in oneself, a radical enmity and irony towards "selflessness," belong as definitely to noble morality, as do a careless scorn and precaution in presence of sympathy and the "warm heart."—It is the powerful who *know* how to honour, it is their art, their domain for invention. The profound reverence for age and for tradition—all law rests on this double reverence,—the belief and prejudice in favour of ancestors and unfavourable to newcomers, is typical in the morality of the powerful; and if, reversely, men of "modern ideas" believe almost instinctively in "progress" and the "future," and are more and more lacking in respect for old age, the ignoble origin of these "ideas" has complacently betrayed itself thereby. A morality of the ruling class, however, is more especially foreign and irritating to present-day taste in the sternness of its principle that one has duties only to one's equals; that one may act towards beings of a lower rank, towards all that is foreign, just as seems good to one, or "as the heart desires," and in any case "beyond good and evil": it is here that sympathy and similar sentiments can have a place. The ability and obligation to exercise prolonged gratitude and prolonged revenge—both only within the circle of equals,—artfulness in retaliation, *raffinement* of the idea in friendship, a certain necessity to have enemies (as outlets for the emotions of envy, quarrelsomeness, arrogance—in fact, in order to be a good *friend*): all these are typical characteristics of the noble morality, which, as has been pointed out, is not the morality of "modern ideas," and is therefore at present difficult to realise and also to unearth and disclose.—It is otherwise with the second type of morality, *slave-morality.* Supposing that the abused, the oppressed, the suffering, the unemancipated, the weary, and those uncertain of themselves, should moralise, what will be the common element in their moral estimates? Probably a pessimistic suspicion with regard to the entire situation of man will find expression, perhaps a condemnation of man, together with his situation. The slave has an unfavourable eye for the virtues of the powerful; he has a scepticism and distrust, a *refinement* of distrust of everything "good" that is there honoured—he would fain persuade himself that the very happiness there is not genuine. On the other hand, *those* qualities which serve to alleviate the existence of sufferers are brought into prominence and flooded with light; it is here that sympathy, the kind, helping hand, the warm heart, patience, diligence, humility, and friendliness attain to honour; for here these are the most useful qualities, and almost the only means of supporting the burden of existence. Slave-morality is essentially the morality of utility.

Here is the seat of the origin of the famous antithesis "good" and "evil":—power and dangerousness are assumed to reside in the evil, a certain dreadfulness, subtlety, and strength, which do not admit of being despised. According to slave-morality, therefore, the "evil" man arouses fear; according to master-morality, it is precisely the "good" man who arouses fear and seeks to arouse it, while the bad man is regarded as the despicable being. The contrast attains its maximum when, in accordance with the logical consequences of slave-morality, a shade of depreciation—it may be slight and well-intentioned—at last attaches itself to the "good" man of this morality; because, according to the servile mode of thought, the good man must in any case be the *safe* man: he is good-natured, easily deceived, perhaps a little stupid, *un bonhomme.* Everywhere that slave-morality gains the ascendency, language shows a tendency to approximate the significations of the words "good" and "stupid."—A last fundamental difference: the desire for *freedom,* the instinct for happiness and the refinements of the feeling of liberty belong as necessarily to slave-morals and morality, as artifice and enthusiasm in reverence and devotion are the regular symptoms of an aristocratic mode of thinking and estimating. –Hence we can understand without further detail why love *as a passion*—it is our European specialty—must absolutely be of noble origin; as is well known, its invention is due to the Provencal poet-cavaliers, those brilliant, ingenious men of the *"gai saber,"* to whom Europe owes so much, and almost owes itself.

PART SIX

VLADIMIR ILYICH LENIN
(1870-1924)

"The Communist Revolution offers peace, land, and bread"

Vladimir Lenin was born in Simbrisk, Russia, in 1870. His father was a school administrator and decidedly of the middle class. Lenin's movement towards revolutionary causes seems to have been fueled by the arrest and execution of his brother Alexander for attempting to assassinate Czar Alexander III in 1887. While studying law at the University of Kazan, Lenin was expelled for revolutionary activities. He briefly practiced law but became absorbed in the teachings of Karl Marx, which he taught to the workers in Saint Petersburg. His actions among the workers were a concern to the Czarist government, and he was exiled to Siberia in 1895. While in exile he wrote *The Development of Capitalism in Russia*, in which he projected the coming of a Communist revolution.

With the outbreak of World War I, Lenin was once again forced into exile for his ringing denunciations of the government. In 1917, shortly after the Czarist government was deposed, Lenin was returned to Russia with the assistance of the German army. Upon arriving in Russia in April, 1917, Lenin delivered his famous *April Theses*, which promoted the Communist promise of revolution and "peace, land, and bread." By November, 1917, Lenin's branch of the Communist Party, known as the Bolsheviks, had succeeded in overthrowing the new provisional government. Lenin then stood as the leader of the new Communist regime in Russia.

Lenin and the Bolsheviks launched what became known as the Red Terror, ousting any and all opposition to his Communist rule. Lenin organized the Third International in 1919 and called for a world revolution to be modeled after Russian Communism. Lenin suffered a stroke in 1922 and ruled with increasingly failing health thereafter. He died in 1924 leaving Russia in the hands of another Bolshevik leader, Joseph Stalin.

(The first World War of the twentieth century was fought on a scale never experienced before. It was a war of mass destruction. In January of 1918, Woodrow Wilson presented his Fourteen Points, *an appeal for peace.)*

The Fourteen Points

We entered this war because violations of right had occurred which touched us to the quick and made the life of our own people impossible unless they were corrected and the world secured once for all against their recurrence. What we demand in this war, therefore, is nothing peculiar to ourselves. It is that the world be made fit and safe to live in; and particularly that it be made safe for every peace-loving nation which, like our own, wishes to live its own life, determine its own institutions, be assured of justice and fair dealing by the other peoples of the world as against force and selfish aggression. All the peoples of the world are in effect partners in this interest, and for our own part we see very clearly that unless justice be done to others it will not be done to us. The program of the world's peace, therefore, is our program; and that program, the only possible program, as we see it, is this:

I. Open covenants of peace, openly arrived at, after which there shall be no private international understandings of any kind but diplomacy shall proceed always frankly and in the public view.

II. Absolute freedom of navigation upon the seas, outside territorial waters, alike in peace and in war, except as the seas may be closed in whole or in part by international action....

III. The removal, so far as possible, of all economic barriers and the establishment of an equality of trade conditions among all nations consenting to the peace and associating themselves for its maintenance.

IV. Adequate guarantees given and taken that national armaments will be reduced to the lowest point consistent with domestic safety.

V. A free, open-minded, and absolutely impartial adjustment of all colonial claims, based upon a strict observance of the principle that in determining all such questions of sovereignty the interests of the populations concerned must have equal weight with the equitable claims of the government whose title is to be determined.

VI. The evacuation of all Russian territory and such a settlement of all questions affecting Russia as will secure the best and freest cooperation of the other nations of the world in obtaining for her an unhampered and unembarrassed opportunity for the independent determination of her own political development and national policy and assure her of a sincere welcome into the society of free nations under institutions of her own choosing; and, more than a welcome, assistance also of every kind that she may need and may herself desire. The treatment accorded Russia by her sister nations in the months to come will be the acid test of their good will, of their comprehension of her needs as distinguished from their own interests, and of their intelligent and unselfish sympathy.

VII. Belgium, the whole world will agree, must be evacuated and restored, without any attempt to limit the sovereignty which she enjoys in common with all other free nations. No other single act will serve as this will serve to restore confidence among the nations in the laws which they have themselves set and determined for the government of their relations with one another. Without this healing act the whole structure and validity of international law is forever impaired.

VIII. All French territory should be freed and the invaded portions restored, and the wrong done to France by Prussia in 1871 in the matter of Alsace-Lorraine, which has unsettled the peace of the world for nearly fifty years, should be righted, in order that peace may once more be made secure in the interest of all.

IX. A readjustment of the frontiers of Italy should be affected along clearly recognizable lines of nationality.

X. The peoples of Austria-Hungary, whose place among the nations we wish to see safeguarded and assured, should be accorded the freest opportunity of autonomous development.

XI. Rumania, Serbia, and Montenegro should be evacuated; occupied territories restored; Serbia accorded free and secure access to the sea; and the relations of the several Balkan states to one another determined by friendly counsel along historically established lines of allegiance and nationality; and international guarantees of the political and economic independence and territorial integrity of the several Balkan states should be entered into.

XII. The Turkish portions of the present Ottoman Empire should be assured a secure sovereignty, but the other nationalities which are now under Turkish rule should be assured an undoubted security of life and an absolutely unmolested opportunity of autonomous development, and the Dardanelles should be permanently opened as a passage to the ships and commerce of all nations under international guarantees.

XIII. An independent Polish state should be erected which should include the territories inhabited by indisputably Polish populations, which should be assured a free and secure access to the sea, and whose political and economic independence and territorial integrity should be guaranteed by international covenant.

XIV. A general association of nations must be formed under specific covenants for the purpose of affording mutual guarantees of political independence and territorial integrity to great and small states alike.

In regard to these essential rectifications of wrong and assertions of right we feel ourselves to be intimate partners of all the governments and peoples associated together against the Imperialists. We cannot be separated in interest or divided in purpose. We stand together until the end.

For such arrangements and covenants we are willing to fight and to continue to fight until they are achieved; but only because we wish the right to prevail and desire a just and stable peace such as can be secured only by removing the chief provocations to war, which this program does remove. We have no jealousy of German greatness, and there is nothing in this program that impairs it. We grudge her no achievement or distinction of learning or of pacific enterprise such as have made her record very bright and very enviable. We do not wish to injure her or to block in any way her legitimate influence or power. We do not wish to fight her either with arms or with hostile arrangements of trade if she is willing to associate herself with us and the other peace-loving nations of the world in covenants of justice and law and fair dealing. We wish her only to accept a place of equality among the peoples of the world,—the new world in which we now live,—instead of a place of mastery.

Neither do we presume to suggest to her any alteration or modification of her institutions.
(From Woodrow Wilson's 1918 speech)

(One of the most important events of the twentieth century was the Russian Revolution of 1917. Its central figure was Lenin. Lenin's return to Russia in April of 1917 was a "turning point" of the Russian Revolution.)

Lenin's April Thesis

- In our attitude towards the war, which under the new government of Lvov and Co. unquestionably remains on Russia's part a predatory imperialist war owing to the capitalist nature of that government, not the slightest concession to a "revolutionary defencism" is permissible....
- The specific feature of the present situation in Russia is that the country is *passing* from the first stage of the revolution – which, owing to the insufficient class-consciousness and organisation of the proletariat, placed power in the hands of the bourgeoisie – to its *second* stage, which must place power in the hands of the proletariat and the poorest sections of the peasants....
- No support for the Provisional Government;...
- Not a parliamentary republic – to return to a parliamentary republic from the Soviets of Workers', Agricultural Labourers' and Peasants' Deputies throughout the country, from top to bottom. Abolition of the police, the army and the bureaucracy. The salaries of all officials, all of who are elective and displaceable at any time, not to exceed the average wage of a competent worker.
- The weight of emphasis in the agrarian programme to be shifted to the Soviets of Agricultural Labourers' Deputies. Confiscation of all landed estates. Nationalisation of *all* lands in the country, the land to be disposed of by the local Soviets of Agricultural Labourers' and Peasants' Deputies. The organisation of separate Soviets of Deputies of Poor Peasants. The setting up of a model farm on each of the large estates (ranging in size from 100 to 300 dessiatines, according to local and other conditions, and to the decisions of the local bodies) under the control of the Soviets of Agricultural Labourers' Deputies and for the public account.

- The immediate amalgamation of all banks in the country into a single national bank, and the institution of control over it by the Soviet of Workers' Deputies.
- . It is not our *immediate* task to "introduce" socialism, but only to bring social production and the distribution of products at once under the *control* of the Soviets of Workers' Deputies.

(From Lenin's April Thesis, 1917)

(Lenin wasted little time in establishing his dictatorship of the Russian people. In January of 1920, he abolished the Constituent Assembly.)

Lenin as Dictator

...The Constituent Assembly, elected on the basis of lists drawn up prior to the October Revolution, was an expression of the old relation of political forces which existed when power was held by the compromisers and the Cadets. When the people at that time voted for the candidates for the Socialist-Revolutionary Party, they were not in a position to choose between the Right Socialist-Revolutionaries, the supporters of the bourgeoisie, and the Left Socialist-Revolutionaries, the supporters of Socialism. Thus the Constituent Assembly, which was to have been the crown of the bourgeois parliamentary republic, could not but become an obstacle in the path of the October Revolution and the Soviet power.

The October Revolution, by giving the power to the Soviets, and through the Soviets to the toiling and exploited classes, aroused the desperate resistance of the exploiters, and in the crushing of this resistance it fully revealed itself as the beginning of the socialist revolution...the majority in the Constituent Assembly which met on January 5 was secured by the party of the Right Socialist-Revolutionaries, the party of Kerensky, Avksentyev and Chernov. Naturally, this party refused to discuss the absolutely clear, precise and unambiguous proposal of the supreme organ of Soviet power, to recognize the "Declaration of Rights of the Toiling and Exploited People," to recognize the October Revolution and the Soviet power....

The Right Socialist-Revolutionary and Menshevik parties are in fact waging outside the walls of the Constituent Assembly a most desperate struggle against the Soviet power....

Accordingly, the Central Executive Committee resolves: The Constituent Assembly is hereby dissolved.
(From Lenin's *Edicts*, 1920)

BENITO MUSSOLINI

(1883-1945)

"Fascism conceives of the State as an absolute, in comparison with which all individuals or groups are relative, only to be conceived of in their relation to the state."

Mussolini was born in North Central Italy in 1883. His father was a blacksmith, his mother a schoolteacher. He was something less than a model student in his youth, having once been expelled for stabbing a fellow student. He eventually earned a diploma and began to teach elementary school in 1901. Mussolini's early political leanings were to the left. He was an ardent student of socialism and read Marx with regularity. He earned a reputation as a flamboyant speaker and advanced quickly in socialist circles. In 1911 Mussolini was jailed for protesting government policies. When he was released in 1912, the Italian Socialist Party appointed him editor of its newspaper *Avanti*.

Italy entered World War I on the allied side in 1915. Breaking with his socialist tradition, Mussolini volunteered for the army and increasingly moved to a nationalist position. He was wounded in battle in 1917 and seems to have denounced his former association with the Socialist Party at this point. After the war Mussolini founded his own party which he named the Fasci Italiani di Combattimento; the members of this group were called Fascists. Mussolini divided his Fascists into armed units known as the Black Shirts. These squads used intimidation as their chief means of obtaining political power. (A method later directly imitated by Adolf Hitler of Germany.)

The end of World War I had brought political chaos to Italy. The Fascists were able to take advantage of this atmosphere and by 1919 thirty-five Fascists, including Benito Mussolini, were elected to the Italian Parliament. By 1922 the Italian government was in a state of crisis. The economy was marked by strikes, food shortages, tax revolts, and widespread anarchy. Mussolini called for a "march on Rome" in order to take over the floundering government. Much to the surprise of Mussolini, people took him at his word and proceeded to march. Startled by the sight of thousands of common people marching on the road to Rome, the Italian government collapsed. Mussolini was invited by the king to create a coalition government with Mussolini serving as prime minister. Between 1922 and 1926 Mussolini created a virtual dictatorship in Italy. His followers began to call him Il Duce, our leader. Mussolini's government collapsed under the strains of World War II, and Mussolini was shot by Italian partisans in 1945.

(Benito Mussolini organized the Fascist Party in 1919. Mussolini, playing heavily on nationalistic themes, called for a total fascist state.)

Mussolini on Fascism

Fascism, the more it considers and observes the future and the development of humanity quite apart from political considerations of the moment, believes neither in the possibility nor the utility of perpetual peace. It thus repudiates the doctrine of Pacifism – born of a renunciation of the struggle and an act of cowardice in the face of sacrifice. War alone brings up to its highest tension all human energy and puts the stamp of nobility upon the peoples who have the courage to meet it....

The Fascist accepts life and loves it, knowing nothing of and despising suicide; he rather conceives of life as duty and struggle and conquest, life which should be high and full, lived for oneself, but above all for other – those who are at hand and those who are far distant, contemporaries, and those who will come after....

Such a conception of life makes Fascism the complete opposite of that doctrine, the base of so-called scientific and Marxian Socialism, the materialist conception of history....Fascism, now and always, believes in holiness and in heroism; that is to say, in actions influenced by no economic motive, direct or indirect....

Fascism repudiates the conception of "economic" happiness, to be realized by Socialism and, as it were, at a given moment in economic evolution to assure to everyone the maximum of well-being. Fascism denies the materialist conception of happiness as a possibility, and abandons it to its inventors, the economists of the first half of the nineteenth century....

After Socialism, Fascism combats the whole complex system of democratic ideology, and repudiates it, whether in its theoretical premises or in its practical application. Fascism denies that the majority, by the simple fact that it is a majority, can direct human society; it denies that numbers alone can govern by means of a periodical consultation, and it affirms the immutable, beneficial, and fruitful inequality of mankind, which can never be permanently leveled through the mere operation of a mechanical process such as universal suffrage....

Fascism denies in democracy, the absurd conventional untruth of political equality dressed out in the garb of collective irresponsibility, and the myth of "happiness" and indefinite progress. But, if democracy may be conceived in diverse forms – that is to say, taking democracy to mean a state of society in which the populace are not reduced to impotence in the State – Fascism may write itself down as "an organized, centralized, and authoritative democracy."

Fascism has taken up an attitude of complete opposition to the doctrines of Liberalism, both in the political field and the field of economics....Fascism uses in its construction whatever elements in the Liberal, Social, or Democratic doctrines still have a living value; it maintains what may be called the certainties which we owe to history, but it rejects all the rest – that is to say, the conception that there can be any doctrine of unquestioned efficacy for all times and all peoples. Given that the nineteenth century was the century of Socialism, of Liberalism, and of Democracy, it does not necessarily follow that the twentieth century must also be a century of Socialism, Liberalism, and Democracy: political doctrines pass, but humanity remains; and it may rather be expected that this will be a century of authority, a century of the Left, a century of Fascism. For if the nineteenth century was a century of individualism (Liberalism always signifying individualism), it may be expected that this will be the century of collectivism, and hence the century of the State. It is a perfectly logical deduction that a new doctrine can utilize all the still vital elements of previous doctrines....

The foundation of Fascism is the conception of the State, its character, its duty, and its aim. Fascism conceives of the State as an absolute, in comparison with which all individuals or groups are relative, only to be conceived of in their relation to the State. The conception of the Liberal State is not that of a directing force, guiding the play and development, both material and spiritual, of a collective body, but merely a force limited to the function of recording results: on the other hand, the Fascist State is itself conscious, and has itself a will and a personality – thus it may be called the "ethic" State....

If every age has its own characteristic doctrine, there are a thousand signs which point to Fascism as the characteristic doctrine of our time. For if a doctrine must be a living thing, this is proved by the fact that Fascism has created a living faith; and that this faith is very powerful in the minds of men, is demonstrated by those who have suffered and died for it.

Fascism has henceforth in the world the universality of all those doctrines which, in realizing themselves, have represented a stage in the history of the human spirit.

(From the *Speeches of Mussolini*, 1919)

WINSTON SPENCER CHURCHILL

(1874-1972)

"From Stettin in the Baltic to Trieste in the Adriatic, an iron curtain has descended across the continent."

Winston Churchill was born in 1874 at Blenheim Palace, his family's ancestral home. His mother Jennie Jerome was American, and his father Randolph Spencer Churchill was a well known British statesman. Winston was a neglected child and seems to have spent a great deal of energy trying to please his father. His father died a painful death from complications relating to syphilis in 1895. After early years of struggle in school, Churchill graduated the Royal Military College at Sandhurst, with honors, in 1895. He was actively involved in military campaigns in Africa between 1895 and 1899. After resigning from the military in 1899, he went to South Africa as a journalist to cover the Boer War, and was subsequently captured by the Dutch. He was able to escape his Boer captors and became something of a folk hero upon his return to England. His exploits helped to propel him to a seat in the House of Commons in 1900.

With the outbreak of World War I, Churchill was appointed first lord of the admiralty, a post he was forced to resign from in 1915 because of his role in the ill-fated campaign in the Dardanelles. Between the wars Churchill found himself temporarily out of public life, but then was elected as a conservative to the House of Commons in 1924. (He would hold this seat for the next forty years.) In the 1930's Churchill began to warn the world of the growing Nazi menace to world peace. After the German invasion of Poland on September 1, 1939, the government led by Prime Minister Neville Chamberlain began to collapse. On May 10, 1940 Churchill was asked by King George VI to become prime minister. Churchill accepted and stated, "I have nothing to offer but blood, toil, tears, and sweat." Despite his personal popularity, his conservative government was defeated at the polls in 1945. He would serve another stint as prime minister in the 1950's.

Between the end of World War II and his second appointment as prime minister, Churchill was preoccupied with the threat of Soviet Communism. In 1946 President Harry S Truman invited Churchill to speak at Westminster College in Fulton, Missouri. This speech became known as the *Iron Curtain Speech*, as Churchill warned of an impenetrable wall of communism surrounding Eastern Europe.

(As the dictatorships of Mussolini and Hitler grew in power, Winston Churchill warned of an impending crisis. In 1938, he warned against "appeasement".)

Churchill on the Munich Agreement

The Chancellor of the Exchequer [Sir John Simon] said it was the first time Herr Hitler had been made to retract–I think that was the word–in any degree. We really must not waste time after all this long Debate upon the difference between the positions reached at Berchtesgaden, at Godesberg and at Munich. They can be very simply epitomized, if the House will permit me to vary the metaphor. One pound was demanded at the pistol's point. When it was given, £2 were demanded at the pistol's point. Finally, the dictator consented to take £1 17s. 6d. and the rest in promise of good will for the future....

I do not grudge our loyal, brave people, who were ready to do their duty no matter what the cost, who never flinched under the strain of last week—I do not grudge them the natural, spontaneous outbursts of joy and relief when they learned that the hard ordeal would no longer be required of them at the moment; but they should know the truth. They should know that there has been gross neglect and deficiency in our defenses; they should know that we have sustained a defeat without a war, the consequences of which will travel far with us along our road; they should know that we have passed an awful milestone in our history, when the whole equilibrium of Europe has been deranged, and that the terrible words have for the time being been pronounced against the Western democracies: "Thou art weighed in the balance and found wanting." And do not suppose that this is the end. This is only the beginning of the reckoning. This is only the first sip, the first foretaste of a bitter cup which will be proffered to us year by year unless, by a supreme recovery of moral health and martial vigor, we rise again and take our stand for freedom as in the olden time.
(From *The Speeches of Churchill*, 1938)

(Winston Churchill was among the first to warn of the Soviet threat after World War II. He delivered his famous "Iron Curtain Speech" at Westminster College in Fulton, Missouri, in 1946.)

Churchill's Iron Curtain Speech (1946)

A shadow has fallen upon the scenes so lately lighted by the Allied victory. Nobody knows what Soviet Russia and its Communist international organization intends to do in the immediate future, or what are the limits, if any, to their expansive and proselytizing tendencies....

From Stettin in the Baltic to Trieste in the Adriatic, an iron curtain has descended across the Continent. Behind that line lie all the capitals of the ancient states of central and eastern Europe. Warsaw, Berlin, Prague, Vienna, Budapest, Belgrade, Bucharest and Sofia; all these famous cities and the populations around them lie in the Soviet sphere and all are subject in one form or another, not only to Soviet influence but to a very high and increasing measure of control from Moscow. Athens alone, with its immortal glories, is free to decide its future at an election under British, American, and French observations. The Russian dominated Polish government has been encouraged to make enormous and wrongful inroads upon Germany, and mass expulsions of millions of Germans on a scale grievous and undreamed of are now taking place. The Communist parties, which were very small in all these eastern states of Europe, have been raised to preeminence and power far beyond their numbers and are seeking everywhere to obtain totalitarian control. Police governments are prevailing in nearly every case, and so far, except in Czechoslovakia, there is no true democracy....

...I do not believe that Soviet Russia desires war. What they desire is the fruits of war and the indefinite expansion of their power and doctrines....

...If the western democracies stand together in strict adherence to the principles of the United Nations Charter, their influence

for furthering these principles will be immense and no one is likely to molest them. If, however, they become divided or falter in their duty, and if these all-important years are allowed to slip away, then indeed catastrophe may overwhelm us all.
(From Churchill's Iron Curtain Speech, 1946)

ADOLF HITLER

(1889-1945)

"It is only a matter of time before we acquire the territory we need. After all, who remembers the extermination of the Armenians?"

Adolf Hitler was born in Branau, Austria, near the German border, in 1889. Hitler's father was prone to beating him, thus driving Hitler into an intense relationship with his mother. When his father died in 1903, the family had enough money to provide a basic education for young Hitler. His mother died in 1908 and seems to have been one of the primary forces in shaping Hitler's personality. He would carry a picture of his mother with him for the rest of his life. Hitler eventually took up the life of an artist and earned a meager living selling his pictures and painted postcards. He applied for entrance into a prestigious art academy in Vienna but was denied on the grounds that his art was not refined. (Hitler had great difficulty drawing the human figure.)

During his artist years, Hitler was exposed to radical antisemitic doctrines on the streets of Vienna. This hatred of the Jewish race, coupled with his faith in the superiority of the Aryan race, would eventually form the basis for his Nazi racial policy. Hitler came to power in Germany in 1933 and almost immediately began a policy of racial division in Germany. In time, these racial policies would cost the lives of over six million Jews throughout Europe.

The fall of Nazi Germany exposed the many facets of Nazi hatred towards the Jewish population and other "undesirables" of Europe. Allied forces chose to hold war crime trials for those Nazis who perpetrated crimes against humanity. The trials were conducted in Nuremberg, the very city where many Nazi doctrines were originally formulated.

(The Nazi party grounded itself in the politics of racial hatred.)

Nazi Racial Policy

Imbued with the knowledge that the purity of German blood is the necessary prerequisite for the existence of the German nation, and inspired by an inflexible will to maintain the existence of the German nation for all future times, the Reichstag has unanimously adopted the following law, which is now enacted:

Article I

1. Any marriages between Jews and citizens of German or kindred blood are herewith forbidden. Marriages entered into despite this law are invalid, even if they are arranged abroad as a means of circumventing this law.
2. Annulment proceedings for marriages may be initiated only by the Public Prosecutor.

Article II

1. Extramarital relations between Jews and citizens of German or kindred blood are herewith forbidden.

Article III

1. Jews are forbidden to employ servants to their households female subjects of German or kindred blood who are under the age of forty-five years.

Article IV

1. Jews are prohibited from displaying the Reich and national flag and from showing the national colors.
2. However, they may display the Jewish colors. The exercise of this right is under state protection.

Article V

1. Anyone who acts contrary to the prohibition noted in Article

I renders himself liable to penal servitude.
2. The man who acts contrary to the prohibition of Article II will be punished by sentence to either a jail or penitentiary.
3. Anyone who acts contrary to the provisions of Articles III and IV will be punished with a jail sentence up to a year and with a fine, or with one of these penalties.

Article VI

1. The Reich Minister of Interior, in conjunction with the Deputy to the F‚hrer and the Reich Minister of Justice, will issue the required legal and administrative decrees for the implementation and amplification of this law.

Article VII

1. This law shall go into effect on the day following its promulgation, with the exception of Article III, which shall go into effect on January 1, 1936.

(From *Nazi Party Documents*, 1936)

(The Nazi Holocaust is estimated to have cost over 6,000,000 Jewish lives. The following is an eyewitness account of the holocaust in Russia.)

A Description of the Holocaust

On October 5, 1942, when I visited the building office at Dubno, my foreman told me that in the vicinity of the site, Jews from Dubno had been shot in three large pits, each about 30 metres long and 3 metres deep. About 1,500 persons had been killed daily. All the 5,000 Jews who has still been living in Dubno before the pogrom were to be liquidated. As the shooting had taken place in his presence, he was still much upset.

Thereupon, I drove to the site accompanied by my foreman and saw near it great mounds of earth, about 30 metres long and 2 metres high. Several trucks stood in front of the mounds. Armed Ukrainian militia drove the people off the trucks under the supervision of an S.S. man. The militiamen acted as guards on the trucks and drove them to and from the pit. All these people had the regulation yellow patches on the front and back of their clothes, and thus could be recognized as Jews.

My foreman and I went directly to the pits. Nobody bothered us. Now I heard rifle shots in quick succession from behind one of the earth mounds. The people who had got off the trucks—men, women and children of all ages—had to undress upon the orders of an S.S. man, who carried a riding or dog whip. They had to put down their clothes in fixed places, sorted according to shoes, top clothing and underclothing. I saw a heap of shoes of about 800 to 1,000 pairs, great piles of underlinen and clothing.

Without screaming or weeping, these people undressed, stood around in family groups, kissed each other, said farewells, and waited for the sign from another S.S. man, who stood near the pit, also with a whip in his hand. During the fifteen minutes that I stood near I heard no complaints or plea for mercy. I watched a family of about eight persons, a man and a woman both about fifty with their children of about one, eight and ten, and two grown-up daughters of about twenty to twenty-nine. An old woman with snow-white hair was holding the one-year-old child in her arms and singing to it and tickling it. The child was cooing with delight. The couple were looking on with tears in their eyes. The father was holding the hand of a boy about ten years old and speaking to him softly; the boy was fighting his tears. The father pointed to the sky, stroked his head, and seemed to explain something to him.

 At that moment the S.S. man at the pit shouted something to his comrade. The latter counted off about twenty persons and instructed them to go behind the earth mound. Among them was the family which I have mentioned. I well remember a girl, slim and with black hair, who, as she passed close to me pointed to herself and said "23". I walked around the mound and found myself confronted by a tremendous grave. People were closely wedged together and lying on top of each other so that only their heads were visible. Nearly all had blood running over their shoulders from their heads. Some of the people shot were still moving. Some were lifting their arms and turning their heads to show that they were still alive. The pit was already two-thirds full. I estimated that it already contained about 1,000 people.
(From *Letters of the Holocaust*, 1945)

HARRY S TRUMAN

(1884-1972)

"One of the primary objectives of the foreign policy of the United States is the creation of conditions in which we and other nations will be able to work out a way of life free of coercion."

Harry S Truman, 33rd president of the United States, was born in Lamar, Missouri, in 1884. When he was six, Truman's family moved to Independence, Missouri, where he obtained his formal education. Upon his graduation from high school in 1901, Truman began a series of jobs and eventually took over the running of the family's farm. When America entered World War I in 1917, Truman enlisted and saw action in France, where he achieved the rank of first lieutenant. Truman entered local politics in Missouri in 1923 by winning an office for county judge. Truman earned a reputation as an honest politician and was elected to the United States Senate in 1934. A consistent New Deal supporter, he was chosen as FDR's running mate in 1944. He ascended to the presidency upon Roosevelt's death in 1945.

As president Truman made the fateful decision to drop the atomic bombs on Hiroshima and Nagasaki, on August 6th and 9th, 1945. After World War II ended, Truman was faced with another dilemma--how to control the aggression of the Soviet Union. Faced with rebuilding a devastated Europe, Truman proposed what became known as the Truman Doctrine of containing communism by spending billions of American dollars to rebuild the economies of Western Europe. Truman, along with Secretary of State George Marshall, launched the Truman Plan soon after the end of the war. It is considered one of the most successful aspects of the Truman presidency.

(In 1947, President Truman announced a plan to contain the threat of Communism. The plan was centered on the use of billions of dollars to rebuild war torn Europe.)

The Truman Doctrine (1947)

I am fully aware of the broad implications involved if the United States extends assistance to Greece and Turkey, and I shall discuss these implications with you at this time.

One of the primary objectives of the foreign policy of the United States is the creation of conditions in which we and other nations will be able to work out a way of life free from coercion. This was a fundamental issue in the war with Germany and Japan. Our victory was won over countries which sought to impose their will, and their way of life, upon other nations.

To insure the peaceful development of nations, free from coercion, the United States has taken a leading part in establishing the United Nations. The United Nations is designed to make possible lasting freedom and independence for all its members. We shall not realize our objectives, however, unless we are willing to help free peoples to maintain their free institutions and their national integrity against aggressive movements that seek to impose upon them totalitarian regimes. This is no more than a frank recognition that totalitarian regimes imposed upon free peoples, by direct or indirect aggression, undermine the foundations of international peace and hence the security of the United States.

The peoples of a number of countries of the world have recently had totalitarian regimes forced upon them against their will. The Government of the United States has made frequent protests against coercion and intimidation, in violation of the Yalta agreement, in Poland, Rumania, and Bulgaria. I must also state that in a number of other countries there have been similar developments.

At the present moment in world history nearly every nation must choose between alternative ways of life. The choice is too often not a free one.

One way of life is based upon the will of the majority, and is distinguished by free institutions, representative government, free elections, guaranties of individual liberty, freedom of speech and religion, and freedom from political oppression.

The second way of life is based upon the will of a minority forcibly imposed upon the majority. It relies upon terror and oppression, a controlled press and radio, fixed elections, and the suppression of personal freedoms.

I believe that it must be the policy of the United States to support free peoples who are resisting attempted subjugation by armed minorities or by outside pressures.

I believe that we must assist free peoples to work out their own destinies in their own way.

I believe that our help should be primarily through economic and financial aid, which is essential to economic stability and orderly political processes.

The world is not static, and the *status quo* is not sacred. But we cannot allow changes in the status quo in violation of the Charter of the United Nations by such methods as coercion, or by such subterfuges as political infiltration. In helping free and independent nations to maintain their freedom, the United States will be giving effect to the principles of the Charter of the United Nations. (From Truman's Speeches, 1947)

NIKITA SERGEYEVICH KHRUSHCHEV

(1894-1971)

"Stalin acted not through persuasion, explanation, and patient cooperation with people, but by imposing his concepts and demanding absolute submission to his opinion."

Nikita Khrushchev was born in southwestern Russia in 1894. His family came from a peasant background; his grandfather had been a serf. Khrushchev had a very limited education and worked as a common laborer until the outbreak of the Russian Civil War in 1918, at which time he became a minor officer in the Red Army. After the Civil War he was appointed to supervise a coal mine in the Ukraine. In 1929 he was appointed to a prestigious Communist Party position in Moscow. In 1939 he became a full member of the Politburo, the Communist Party's primary decision-making group.

Khrushchev was able to move up through the ranks of the Communist Party by exhibiting a strong loyalty to Joseph Stalin. By 1949 Khrushchev was one of the most influential leaders within the Communist Party. When Stalin died in 1953, Khrushchev became head of the party. The Stalinist years were marked by constant political purges and intrigues. Millions of Soviet citizens had perished during this period. Despite his direct connection to the Stalinist regime, Khrushchev, upon taking power, began what has become known as the "de-Stalinization" of Russia. In 1956 he delivered a secret speech to the Communist Party Congress denouncing Stalin's tactics. After 1956 the wholesale use of purges as a political tool began to wane. Stalin was essentially removed from the history books of Russia.

Khrushchev ruled until 1964. During his years in office he became the very symbol of Cold War politics. He ordered the building of the Berlin Wall in 1961, and along with John Kennedy, he brought the world to the brink of nuclear war in 1962. He later opened the door for dÈtente in the post missile crisis era of 1963. In the end Khrushchev was forced from his office, more because of his failure to solve the economic problems of Russia, than for his handling of foreign policy.

(In 1956, Kruschev denounced the crimes of Joseph Stalin. Kruschev himself had once served under Stalin.)

Kruschev Denounces Stalin

Stalin acted not through persuasion, explanation, and patient cooperation with people, but by imposing his concepts and demanding absolute submission to his opinion. Whoever opposed this concept or tried to prove his viewpoint and the correctness of his position was doomed to removal from the leading collective [group] and to subsequent moral and physical annihilation....

Stalin originated the concept of "enemy of the people." This term automatically rendered it unnecessary that the ideological errors of a man or men engaged in a controversy be proved; this term made possible the usage of the most cruel repression violating all norms of revolutionary legality, against anyone who in any way disagreed with Stalin, against those who were only suspected of hostile intent, against those who had bad reputations.

This concept "enemy of the people" actually eliminated the possibility of any kind of ideological fight or the making of one's views known on this or that issue, even those of a practical character. In the main, and in actuality, the only proof of guilt used, against all norms of current legal science, was the "confession" of the accused himself; and, as a subsequent probing proved, "confessions" were acquired through physical pressures against the accused....

Lenin used severe methods only in the most necessary cases, when the exploiting classes were still in existence and were vigorously opposing the revolution, when the struggle for survival was decidedly assuming the sharpest forms, even including civil war.

Stalin, on the other hand, used extreme methods and mass repressions at a time when the revolution was already victorious, when the Soviet State was strengthened, when the exploiting classes were already liquidated and the Socialist relations were rooted solidly in all phases of national economy, when our party was politically consolidated and had strengthened itself both numerically and ideologically. It is clear that here Stalin showed in a whole series of cases his intolerance, his brutality, and his abuse of power. In-

stead of proving his political correctness and mobilizing the masses, he often chose the path of repression and physical annihilation, not only against actual enemies, but also against individuals who had not committed any crimes against the party and the Soviet Government....
(From Kruschev's speeches, 1956)

50 Great Paintings

1. *The Mona Lisa* by Leonardo da Vinci
2. *Girl With an Ermine* by Leonardo da Vinci
3. *The Last Supper* by Leonardo da Vinci
4. *The Sistine Chapel* by Michelangelo
5. *The School of Athens* by Raphael
6. *Venus de Urbino* by Titian
7. *Adam and Eve* by Durer
8. *The Hare* by Durer
9. *The Crucifixion* by Grunewald
10. *Paradise and Hell* by Bosch
11. *Madonna with the Long Neck* by Parmigianino
12. *The Birth of the Milky Way* by Tintoretto
13. *View of Toledo* by El Greco
14. *Brother Hortensio* by El Greco
15. A *German Merchant* by Hans Holbein
16. *Peasant Wedding* by Bruegel
17. *Hunters in the Snow* by Bruegel
18. *Doubting Thomas* by Caravaggio
19. *The Conversion of St. Paul* by Caravaggio
20. *'Et Arcardia Ego'* by Poussin
21. *Landscapes With Sacrifice to Apollo* by Claude Lorrain
22. *Virgin and Child* by Rubens
23. *Self Portrait* by Rubens
24. *Charles I of England* by Van Dyck
25. *Las Meninas* by Velasquez
26. *The Laughing Cavalier* by Frans Hals
27. *Self Portraits* by Rembrandt
28. *The Reconciliation of David and Absalom* by Rembrandt
29. *The Kitchen Maid* by Jan Vermeer
30. *View of Delft* by Jan Vermeer
31. *Girl With a Pearl Earring* by Jan Vermeer
32. *The Swing* by Fragonard
33. *Still Life* by Chardin
34. *Pierrot* by Watteau

35. *Departure from the Isle of Cythera* by Watteau
36. *Oath of the Horatii* by David
37. *Death of Socrates* by David
38. *Death of Marat* by David
39. *The Raft of the Medussa* by Gericault
40. *Portrait of a Child Murderer* by Gericault
41. *The Third of May* by Goya
42. *Saturn Devouring His Children* by Goya
43. *Liberty Leading the People* by Delacroix
44. *Napoleon I* by Ingres
45. *The Odalisque* by Ingres
46. *Abbey Under the Oak Trees* by Caspar David Friedrich
47. *The Fighting Temperaire* by Turner
48. *Rain, Steam, and Speed* by Turner
49. *The Hay Wain* by Constable
50. *The Gleaners* by Millet

10 GREAT COMPOSERS

Composer	Musical Period	Life Span
1. Antonio Vivaldi	Baroque	1678-1741
2. Johann Sebastian Bach	Baroque	1685-1750
3. George Handel	Baroque	1685-1759
4. Franz Haydn	Classical	1732-1809
5. Wolfgang Amadeus Mozart	Classical	1756-1791
6. Ludwig Van Beethoven	Classical	1770-1827
7. Frederic Chopin	Early Romantic	1810-1849
8. Richard Wagner	Early Romantic	1813-1883
9. Franz Liszt	Early Romantic	1811-1886
10. Johannes Brahms	Middle Romantic	1833-1897

75 Words to Study History With

1. Extant
2. Empirical
3. Truculent
4. Dowry
5. Usury
6. Secular
7. Vernacular
8. Humanism
9. Nascent
10. Stigmata
11. Theocracy
12. Sycophant
13. Amoral
14. Pious
15. Catholic
16. Bohemian
17. Liturgy
18. Austere
19. Nefarious
10. Bard
21. Gentry
22. Divergent
23. Patronage
24. Refractory
25. Regency
26. Epistemology
27. Inalienable
28. Liberal
29. Truncate
30. Philanderer
31. Hegemony
32. Chiaroscuro
33. Mannerism
34. Naturalism
35. Genre
36. Prolific
37. Virtuoso
38. Concerto
39. Puritanical
40. Ribald
41. Canon
42. Reactionary
43. Axiom
44. Contiguous
45. Usurp
46. Vestiges
47. Refractory
48. Megalomania
49. Acumen
50. Sedition
51. Intemperate
52. Specter
53. Manifesto
54. Hiatus
55. Permeate
56. Rescind
57. Malefactor
58. Obfuscate

59. Sobriquet
60. Draconian
61. Anathema
62. Malinger
63. Covert
64. Animism
65. Antebellum
66. Apologia
67. Archetype

68. Barcarole
69. Basilica
70. Bawdy
71. Behemoth
72. Boudoir
73. Callow
74. Cartel
75. Conjecture

www.ingramcontent.com/pod-product-compliance
Lightning Source LLC
Chambersburg PA
CBHW071144160426
43196CB00011B/2007